397 CHAIRS

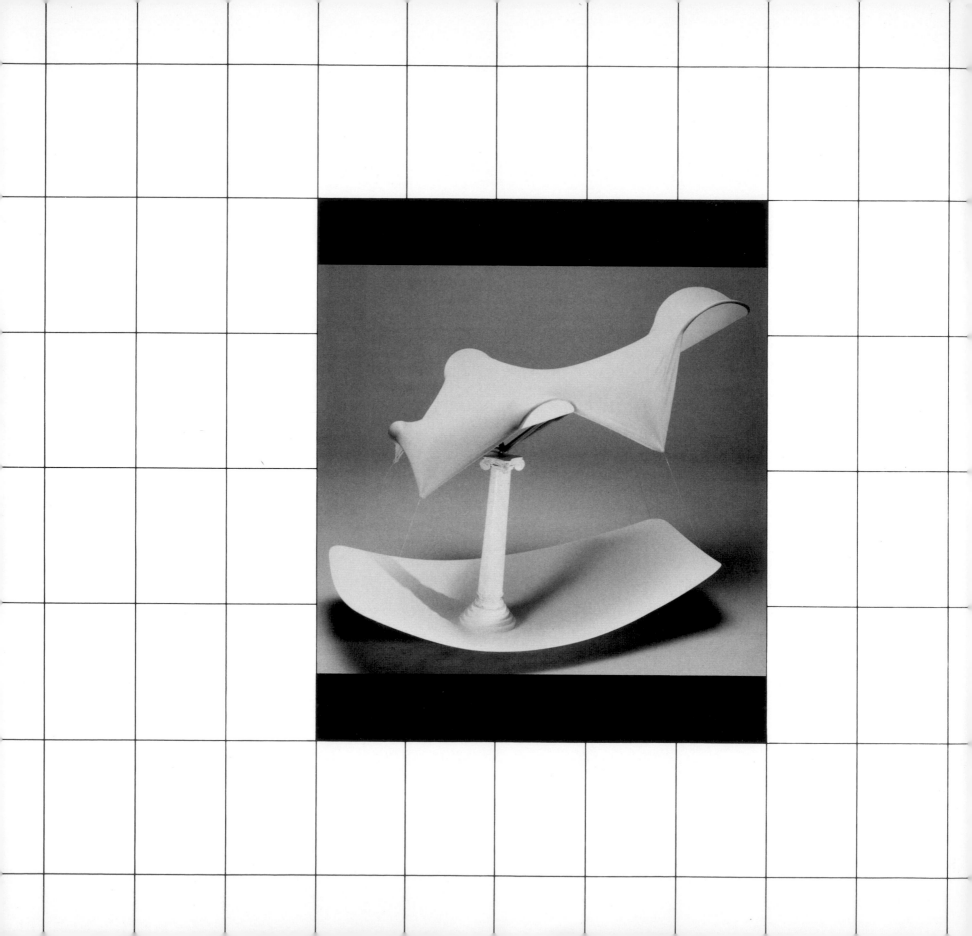

397 CHAIRS

Essay by Arthur C. Danto

Photographs by Jennifer Lévy

Based on an exhibition created by
The Architectural League
of New York

HARRY N. ABRAMS, INC., PUBLISHERS, NEW YORK

Project Director: Robert Morton
Art Director: Samuel N. Antupit
Design Assistant: Doris Leath

Library of Congress Cataloging-in-Publication Data

Danto, Arthur Coleman, 1924–
397 chairs.
"Based on an exhibition created by the Architectural League of New York."
1. Chairs—United States—History—20th century—Exhibitions.
2. Architect-designed furniture—United States—Exhibitions.
I. Lévy, Jennifer. II. Architectural League of New York.
III. Three hundred ninety-seven chairs. IV. Title.
NK2408.D36 1988   749′.32′07401471   88–942
ISBN 0–8109–1698–3

A Times Mirror Company
Printed and bound in Japan

397 CHAIRS

CONTENTS

PREFACE

This book is based on "The Chair Fair," an exhibition organized by The Architectural League of New York, which for over a hundred years has been a meeting place for artists, architects, and designers. At the League, we had noticed that numerous established architects—Robert Venturi, Richard Meier, Michael Graves, and others—were designing chairs, often at the invitation of furniture manufacturers. Young architects also were designing chairs, and, of course, so were craftsmen in various disciplines. Artists were designing chairs, and so, naturally, were professional furniture makers. Each group seemed to have a different theory about what they were doing, yet all were concerned in some way with the creation of perhaps the most ubiquitous household object.

We decided to get a great many of these chairs together, to provide a common ground for evaluating and comparing them.

Our exhibition was open to anyone who wanted to send in a chair. But first we needed to define a chair. In this, artist and League board member Richard Artschwager was most helpful: "If it looks like a chair," he reasoned, "it might be one. If you can sit in it, it is." With this simple criterion, models of chairs, drawings of chairs, and all chairlike objects which could not be sat in, were excluded from the exhibition. Our only other ground rules were that the chairs had to have been designed and made during the past ten years, and that they would be exhibited in the order in which they arrived, on the model of a State Fair.

All the chairs that could be seen in the exhibition can be seen again here. And as our viewers did, each reader can make his or her own assessment of which ones are artful, which ones especially embody the nature of "chairness," and which are simply wonderful inventions. Each viewer can, for a moment, escape from preconceptions, return to the objects themselves, and perhaps begin to speculate on function, form, design, and utility.

Many people and organizations helped realize the project. First, we thank Milton Glaser, who listened to our initial plans and had the wit to say, "Why don't you call it Chair Fair?" Fern Mallis invited us to stage the exhibition at The International Design Center in New York, and she and Liz Bruder of IDCNY provided continuing help and encouragement. Domore Corporation, Herman Miller, Inc., Knoll International, Steelcase Inc., Atelier International, Furniture Consultants, Inc., The Gunlocke Company, and

SunarHauserman shared our enthusiasm and contributed generously. At the League, a committee of Milton Glaser, Richard Artschwager, and Henry Altchek provided continuing guidance. Rosalie Genevro, the League's Executive Director, and Christopher Flacke, Chair Fair Project Director, worked tirelessly to sort out a myriad details without misplacing anything.

A panel of five jurors selected five prize-winning chairs. The *Tonietta Chair* (262), by Enzo Mari, was chosen for its spare elegance. Philippe Starck's *Cafe Costes Chair* (263) seemed to the judges to reinterpret successfully a classic type, the tub chair. The *Derecktor Chair* (156), by Derecktor Furniture, appealed to the judges for the straightforward way in which a beautiful wood was worked and finished, and for the simplicity of the form. The *Pool Chair* (178), by Steven Holt, Tucker Viemeister, and Lisa Krohn, was chosen for the playfulness of its metaphor and the consistency with which the conceit was carried through. And an unnamed chair (309), built on the spot by Tom Musorafita, a construction worker at the IDCNY, was compared by the judges to a flight of jazz improvisation that captured the essence of chair with economical means and in a minimum of time.

The jurors were artist Richard Artschwager, architect and industrial designer Mario Bellini, graphic designer Milton Glaser, sculptor and architect Tim Prentice, and furniture and graphic designer Lella Vignelli.

Arthur Danto's essay, "The Seat of the Soul," was originally presented as a lecture at the exhibition. Although Mr. Danto had previously had no connection with the Architectural League—nor with the design or manufacture of chairs—we had read him in *The Nation* and felt a kinship with his defining art in its cultural context and his good-natured affection for everyday things. We are delighted to share his perceptions about chairs with a wider audience here.

Finally, we thank the designers, makers, and sponsors of the 397 chairs for helping us to preserve this moment of design history.

Frances Halsband
President, The Architectural League of New York

The Chair Fair Award.
Designed by Milton Glaser
and fabricated by Nicholas Fasciano

I·sing the sofa. I, who lately sang
Truth, Hope, and Charity, and touch'd with awe
The solemn chords. . . .
William Cowper

For some years, the official correspondence of the Philosophy Department of Columbia University went out over my signature—scrawled, inimitable, urgent, illegible—

securely situated above my clearly lettered title: Chair. In the letterhead universe of officialdom, the seated signature is universally recognized as the mark of power and authority—so instantly acknowledged a symbol that I have often wondered why artists who traffic in punning interchanges between sign and reality, Magritte, for example, should never have produced the artwork of my dreams, consisting of the curvaceous horizontal signature

elongated atop CHAISE LONGUE

in suitably elegant Empire majuscules.

In the spirit of such symbolism, when it was important that my status be stressed, the signature went out spread across two chairs, one referring to my stewardship of that crew of scholars and contenders that composes the philosophy department, the other to the distinction conferred upon me as the occupant of the Johnsonian Chair in Philosophy.

The academic chair has a long history that takes us back to the medieval origins of the university as we know it, where it would have been designated, in Latin, as *cathedra*. Even now, when one speaks with the weight and authority of one's position in a relevant hierarchy, one speaks *ex cathedra*—from the chair. The cathedra was the bishop's seat, and like my two-chaired title, it carried administrative and doxological authority. The term cathedra itself derives from two Greek words—*katha* (down) and *hedra* (seat)—a redundancy, it seems to me, as if, by saying the same thing in two different ways, one draws rhetorical attention, like underlining a word twice, to the object being designated, just as the cathedral itself—majestic, soaring, standing against the sky like a filigreed exclamation point—draws attention to the bishop's chair it symbolizes. It is as if only a structure that awesome is fit to symbolize the chair that is its *raison d'être*.

So the chair has a locus in the language of authority as a mark and perquisite of power. To remain seated while others stand is to enact, bodily, the possession of superior value. Standing, while someone else remains seated, is to acquiesce in the sitter's authority, and should the latter rise—to put himself, as the expression goes, on an equal footing with the stander—he raises the other in raising himself. "Please rise," as a ministerial imperative, when we are summoned to pray or show respect, is the postural synonym for kneeling in the language of deference. Kneeling is itself to offer onself *as a chair*—and it is not a matter for surprise that there existed, in ancient times, chairs designed in the form of slaves or conquered enemies. (In the Chair Fair, I saw a seat with the portrait, unmistakable, of Richard Nixon, which celebrates exactly this meaning.)

Bowing or curtsying are momentary acknowledgments of subservience by assuming the fleeting form of something that might be sat on. (*Serviteur*, the courtier murmurs as he executes a *révérence*.) After a bow, we immediately revert to the vertical posture in which we may be joined by one who was seated, in the event that we are to be paid the compliment of that person standing. No chairholder, I should think, would ever confer equal status by joining another in the kneeling position, save as in the presence of a higher authority before whom gradations are erased. But to acknowledge a bow with a bow is of a piece with standing up with the already standing.

The act of ennoblement takes place when the candidate first kneels, then receives the touch, then complies with the order to "Arise as Sir Launcelot!," the Ennobler all the while remaining seated. The Ennobler may at that point rise, conferring respect, and giving the other the right to take a seat at the Round Table. The order of seating, as at banquets or on the dais of authority, where right and left replace up and down with respect to a fixed center, gives precise equivalences in the medium of furniture arrangements to the structures of power that define society or even the cosmos. The seated position implies stability, solidity, the unmoved center around which the remainder of the universe orbits.

The degree to which the nobility of the Sun's light and kingliness suggested, as a politico-astronomical necessity, to the early believers in the heliostatic theory, that it was appropriate for the Sun to be the center of things cannot be too heavily stressed. There it was, enthroned, still and unwobbling, holding the lesser planets in their whizzing paths by the mysterious operation of action-at-a-distance, not even doing anything to keep them in their place. It was altogether appropriate that it should have been called the Copernican Revolution—unseating what went before by way of usurpation of the place of power by a mere lump of mud—though it might be even more appropriately called the Copernican Restoration, given the cosmopolitical assumptions which we reenforce each time we stand or sit in one another's presence.

If, to the academic chair and the episcopal *cathedra*, we add the regal throne, the judicial bench, the congressional seat, it is clear that the chair itself occupies the place of preeminence in the community of pieces of basic furniture, each of which corresponds to the animal needs they transfigure and ritualize. This is because, so far as I know, none of the others—tables or beds, to take the obvious examples—are said to rule, or judge, or decide, or determine, as the chair, the throne, the bench are said and expected to do. I am uncertain why this is so, but I am disinclined to accept an explanation through bodily posture, as opposed to position.

There is a notorious chair, associated with but evidently not invented by the Marquis de Sade, which served him as an aid to abrupt seduction: some system of springs tripped the back legs, so that the unsuspecting woman who assumed the sitting posture would find herself rotated into the passive position of the so-called act of love, where her mental attitude, according to Sade's psychology, would be more or less "What the hell, as long as I'm on my back..." The recognition that the sitting posture and the passive sexual position should be rotations through ninety degrees of one another was the sort of thing that recommended itself to an erotic geometrist like Sade. Though orientation must have counted heavily in his psychology—the *seated* woman would not have said "What the hell..."—I am sufficiently impressed by the essential congruence of the two positions to discount posture, that is to say, the deployment of limbs, as the explanation of the chair's political preeminence. My sense, rather, is that it connects with notions of freedom and dignity.

The bed and the table are used regularly and recurrently in obedience to the body's rhythms. We eat and sleep at regular times, symbolic of our oneness with the natural material order of the world. The bed and table are empty when not in use—with sickness and lovemaking being states of the same order as sleeping, so far as autonomy or freedom are concerned. We employ the chair at any time and to no set purpose, and our human dignity is celebrated by its existence as an article of furnishing. To be sure, there are bodily functions discharged while seated, or more primitively while squatting, but my speculation is that since these in fact can be exercised through the squat, the chair serves to symbolize that acts of elimination are under our control. In any case, there is, apart from this, no specific natural function with which the chair is associated, and as the one article of furniture with no preordained use it is a natural or obvious symbol of freedom, which is the political corollary of power.

The chair has been available for human use and hence for philosophical metaphor for some five millennia, and I am struck that it is the sitting position that is spontaneously invoked in the philosophy of mind when one speaks of the *seat* of the soul, or of intelligence, or of wisdom or reason. Descartes spoke of the pineal gland, a mysterious organ suspended like the seat of Breuer's Wassily chair midway between the cerebral hemispheres, as the seat of the thinking essence of man. A bed would have been inappropriate for the soul which, in his philosophy, *always* thinks and *never* sleeps. And what would the soul do with a table? (Locke, to be sure, spoke of the mind as a blank table—a tabula rasa—but that was the mind as the passive recipient of experience, and had nothing to do with reason or intelligence.) Memory might naturally suggest a chest or cupboard. But a seat seems altogether appropriate, given the psycho-political analogies that have been felt to be compelling since Plato, where reason rules the individual as the philosopher rules society. To rule, decide, judge, which are the functions of the soul in Descartes—or to withhold judgment when circumstance mandates circumspection—the soul must be able from its seat to survey left and right like the bishop (a word which, in its Greek form of *episcope*, means to look around or survey) in his cathedra, the magistrate on his bench, the king on his throne. In any case, the chair leaves the senses free for thought and its higher labors. Jerome, the one saint with any claim to intellect in contrast with mere faith or fervor, is standardly represented as seated (the bed would be no place to translate the Pentateuch), though admittedly he is peering into some heavy volume propped up on his scholar's table. But this only underscores the great versatility of the chair, sometimes drawn up to the table for this or that pursuit, but capable of uses of its own. It rests the body, leaving its higher faculties to pursue their more elevated concerns.

Whatever the merits of these speculations, they acknowledge the point of thinking about chairs philosophically to begin with. To think that an object so connected with authority, domination, autonomy, and power is to be construed simply in terms of *comfort* would be equivalent to thinking that sex—the activity through which so many of the relationships are defined in which we stand to one another, to the tribe, and to the surrounding forces of the universe—is to be appreciated solely in terms of pleasure. This is to deny neither the importance of comfort or of pleasure, but only to insist that when these become the central considerations in thinking about sitting and sex respectively, a transformation in human meaning will have taken place in which comfort and pleasure themselves have acquired a meaning quite beyond what they possess in themselves. Sartre once said, with characteristic brilliance, that we are not sexual beings because we have sexual organs but—on the contrary—that we have sexual attributes because we are deeply, ontologically, in our ultimate nature, sexual beings; that sexuality is our being-in-the-world, the moral center around which the entirety of life is radiated with meaning. To change the meaning of sex, then, is to change the whole tone and color of the rest of existence, construed as a system of meanings. And then to reduce all this to pleasure is to erase and rewrite what it means to be human, responsive, responsible; to change the meaning of agreeing or refusing physical relationship; to change the point and significance of fidelity, chastity, trust (if all it is is pleasure, why not get it where we can?), to transfer sexual identity from our central essence to an attribute of recreation and leisure. And so I think it is, less momentously but no less certainly, with sitting down, less as a matter of taking weight off our feet than one of declaring where we are and how we fit in the larger scheme of things. So when the chair becomes an instrument of comfort, it is not as though it loses its political or social meaning, but rather that it acquires a different one.

The English wing chair, in which we sit protected, and alone, and enclosed, facing the warmth of the fire, embraced by wings as if those of a soft sheltering angel, implies a different form of life and a different set of values altogether from the precarious and portable salon chair of France, meant to be carried from place to place, from conversing group to conversing group, or to be arranged for a party of whist, or in a circle surrounding a string trio, and implying an essential sociability. In it, one's arms are free to gesticulate, one does not settle but sits, posed on its edge, like a bird, ready for the flights that are analogous to conversation. The salon chair's lightness and elegance stipulate the form of life to which it is organically connected; the wing chair's heaviness and solidity stipulate a different form of life—one of security, of solidity, of immobility, of peace. It is not an accident that Sade should see the salon chair in terms of seduction, or think of it as treacherous and betraying. The wing chair goes with the bourgeois interior, the hearth, with an Englishman's home being his castle. The sitter is padded, buffered, cosseted, soothed. One's chair is one's signature.

Perhaps this suffices as justification for treating the chair as something more than where we place our bottoms, and I want now to speak of the chair in artistic representations before going on to speak of the chair *as* art, or as an art form in its own right. My sense is that some of the meanings the chair in art has, and which make it so compelling a symbolic presence, are repudiated when the chair is treated as an occasion for artistic expression. The chair *in,* as opposed to *as,* art is deeply connected with the kinds of considerations I have just sought to articulate, where its use conveys—eloquently in the cases I mean to present—propositions it would be difficult to convey propositionally. I am anxious to present some images of chairs taken as vehicles of meaning to which their nature as chairs is crucial, but where the meaning goes quite beyond what we would think a mere chair capable of, taken simply as an article of furniture.

The Assault of Mara,
Amaravati, 2nd Century A.D.
Courtesy Madras Museum

Thus I am interested in chairs here not as incidental illustrations, such as we find in Mario Praz's magnificent volume on the history of furnishing, nor in those wonderful painted portraits of domestic interiors that visitors to the Thaw Collection at the Morgan Library might have seen—a minor but charming genre which the Thaws have taken up as a specialty, and with which, you will recall, Charles Ryder, the hero of Evelyn Waugh's novel *Brideshead Revisited,* made his reputation. Even in these portraits, the chair is not innocent of meaning. But the meanings it expresses are expressed equally well by the draperies and carpets, the lamps and hangings, the pictures or carvings; it expresses in the first instance the taste of the owners, their social status, and the times in which they enjoyed it. Even then, in the complex conversation between the furnishings, one might be able to identify the specific voice of the chair, what it meant in relationship to the other items—a relationship that varies from age to age and even from interior to interior. There is that sense in which the furnishings of a room are a system of signs and, indeed, in one of my examples I shall mean to focus specifically on this. But I am interested in chairs that transcend the meanings they are confined to in such a system, where they rise to eloquence in contexts more dramatic than that of domestic interiors, and where they sound meanings of the deepest order. What I am, after all, bent on is the revelation of the chair in systems of meaning of the widest human consequence.

Let me begin, then, with a very early representation of a chair, a relief sculpture from the ruined Buddhist stupa of Amaravati, which dates from the second century A.D. The subject of this relief is a set piece in Buddhist iconography, much as the Crucifixion or the Last Judgment are set pieces in the Christian epic. It shows the Assault of Mara, the Hindu-Buddhist god of death who is also, under another name, Kama, the god of pleasure, and especially of sexual pleasure. This linking of sexual desire and death in a single entity is, of course, familiar in the West in the tale of Tristan and Isolde, specifically in the *Liebestod*—the Love Death—that admirers of Wagner are so moved by. And it is in both dimensions of his being that Mara-Kama is making an assault on the Buddha at a critical moment in the story of the Buddha's quest for Enlightenment. The moment is critical because Buddha is not yet the Buddha, but still only the Prince Gautama, and the great change—for which mankind is grateful—is the change from prince to saint or even deity, though Buddha himself never spoke of himself in terms appropriate to a god. His message, after all, was that what he achieved was something we can all achieve, and hence his essential humanity was essential to his revelation. It was because we can in some measure follow the arduous path laid out by the Buddha, that we ourselves can rise above death and distraction, transcend the ultimate limits of our fleshly selves, and hence slip the powers of Mara-Kama, bringing his dominion to an end. No wonder Mara-Kama senses the momentousness of the episode in which Gautama achieved

Buddhahood, which, as you know, transpired through a seance of the most intense contemplation under the now sacred Bo Tree, in Patna.

Let us examine the Amaravati sculpture: the relief, bisected by the Bo Tree itself, is almost perfectly symmetrical. To what would be the Prince's right are threatening figures, carrying frightening things. A verbal description of the scene calls for a "mighty host…causing mighty storms of wind, showers of rain, flaming rocks, weapons, live coals, hot ashes, sand, boiling mud, and finally a great darkness to assail him." The discrepancy between these words and what a sculptor is capable of showing is, of course, pathetically in favor of speech. But the frieze of elephants, those emblems of savage strength, gives us iconic equivalences not at all contemptible. On the Prince's left is a chorus of provocative, swaying women, heavy-breasted and heavy-hipped, like Edwardian beauties. Their arms are behind their heads to raise their breasts to prominence, and a naughty tassel swings between their legs. They symbolize what Heinrich Zimmer called the "world's supreme distraction." A man who can stand up against these can stand up against anything—but the Buddha is seated. Or rather he *was* seated. The chair is empty. He has transcended that dimension of his being which can be threatened by demons or drawn toward women. I know of no more powerful a representation of transcendence than the empty throne in this great relief. It bears comparison in religious strength to the staggering *Resurrection* of Piero della Francesca in Borgo San Sepolcro, in my view the greatest painting of Christendom.

I want to meditate on that empty throne for a moment, and draw out some of its meaning. I have been at great pains to stress the cosmic drama in which this chair plays its role, partly as an example of the way in which this article of furniture fits into schemes of meaning well beyond those of decoration, and partly to draw attention to the fact that the chair makes palpable, exactly as Gregory the Great demanded artists do, the deep truths of existence. To begin with, it is very much the chair of Prince Gautama, rather than the enlightened Buddha, who is rarely pictured thereafter in chairs at all. He is always, or typically, when shown seated, shown in the posture of contemplation—the lotus position—beyond the need for chairs. He is self-contained, in effect not needing an external locus of authority, and I suppose the *absence* of a chair for the seated Buddha, as much as anything, implies his self-containedness: he is in effect seated nowhere, much as, I suppose, were we to represent God, we would not place him in a chair. (Christ is pictured seated, often, but that connects with his being *human*.) On Gautama's chair is a cushion, left behind; a terribly touching detail. It belongs to that kind of being who can be frightened by injury, or death, or drawn erect by the sexual presence of women. Comfort is not something that belongs to the Buddha, but to the Prince. But it certainly underscores his royalty. He was a very cosseted and protected prince, who never knew that pain existed until he one day walked out of the pleasure gardens which defined his world, and seeing death, old age, disease, embarked upon that itinerary of meditation that climaxed under the Bo Tree.

My sense is that the comfortable chair, the chair with cushions, must have emblemized the soft life of the ruler: courtiers and commoners must have sat on harder chairs, or even stools and taborets, as in the hierarchies of sitting modalities for which the court at Versailles was celebrated. A profound social revolution is marked when the comfort is transferred from the cushions and paddings, even the coiled springs of the upholstered chair, to the structure of the chair itself, which becomes comfortable through its architectural form. I refer to the cantilevered rocker, invented, I believe, in 1851 in England by R. G. Winfield. Even without upholstery, or perhaps just because it lacks upholstery, the cantilevered rocker displays its comfort in its form. It is almost an impossible exercise of social imagination to suppose that the rocker could have been invented in France, despite the tradition of *liberté, égalité, fraternité*, or in nineteenth-century Germany. The chair implies a democratic society, where each is entitled to the comfort reserved previously for princes.

The cantilevered chair, of course, took a tremendous surge in the 1920s when its tubular frame, chromium plated, became the symbol of modernity; here, the point about structural comfort is taken for granted, so one can use cushions with symbolic impunity. In 1986, at the Mies van der Rohe show at the Museum of Modern Art in New York, while studying Mies's own Brno cantilevered chair of 1930—so emblematic of contemporaneity—I was reminded, with the force of a Proustian revelation, of an episode in my own childhood. My father, a dentist, changed the style of his waiting room from tan walls, musty chairs, and rickety tables to what my parents referred to, proudly, as "modernesque." I remember vividly my brother and I being taken to see the snappy new room, and encouraged to sit—we were not to worry, it was perfectly safe despite there being no back legs—we would not tip backward. So we sat gingerly, bounced up and down tentatively, and felt terrifically up-to-date.

The day I studied Mies's chair, of which my father's proud furnishings were knock-offs, I thought that what gave my parents the sense of modernity was precisely the implied risk in sitting in a chair with too little visible support. And it then occurred to me that the chair carried a fragment of the same *Zeitgeist* as another innovation of the 1930s, the strapless evening gown, regarded as a daring thing in its day, but almost certainly as safe in its buttressed security as the Mies chair was in the principle of the cantilever. It was the most delicious combination of risk and certitude that made those chairs so appealing to those whose consciousness was continuous with that of my parents.

There is another feature of Gautama's chair that merits attention: the legs. The legs are heavily curved, and bowed out—but not in the sense in which the familiar cabriole legs of Queen Anne furniture are bowed. Indeed, the legs of Gautama's chair resemble the legs of a man under tremendous pressure to lift a great weight from a squatting position. The bow of the legs reflects on the weight and hence importance of the princely house to which Gautama belongs, and it carries the message of domination. It is a very political message, indeed, and clearly belongs to the world Buddha must have rejected and which Gautama himself precociously rejected. But it is part of the language of the chair that one has power over what one sits on. There are some terribly funny medieval effigies of the philosopher Aristotle on all fours with a young and reckless woman on his back, as though he were a horse. This perverse juxtaposition between Phyllis (the mistress of Alexander the Great) and Aristotle—whom Dante designates *il Maestro di color che sanno*—is the realization of a masochistic fantasy, or perhaps a philosophical allegory of how passion dominates reason. But it is crucial to its meaning that it should be Aristotle, the tutor to the conqueror of the world, who supports a girl as willful and frivolous as Salome. She celebrates her own power by dominating a man more powerful than she: what one sits on *must* be more powerful than oneself if the domination is to mean something. So the legs on the Gautama's chair must themselves belong to a powerful being, a conquered warrior, perhaps a conquered king, or possibly a giant—domesticated and made to feel our weight, which is negligible, save as metaphor, in the case of pretty Phyllis.

The cabriole legs of Queen Anne furniture emblemize the elegantly curved foreleg of the prancing horse, a horse trained and bred to aristocratic ends—not the plug, not the plowhorse, not the spavined and heavy-legged horse of the parson, but the exact and delicate foreleg of the thoroughbred animal. Thus, in the drawing room itself the mounted postures of the privileged class are reenacted. But legs have almost always, in great furniture design, conveyed some such message: the heavily clawed and pawed feet imply an animal realm of savage beasts, of wild and menacing animals, and in sitting upon them we underscore our human superiority. These animate metaphors have disappeared from chair design, and today have given way to supports of a different order, but by no means to a less symbolic order. There was an exhibit of modern chairs that bore the title *La machine à s'asseoir*, clearly and wittily derived from the famous definition of the ideal house by Le Corbusier. And this, indeed, makes it seem as though the chair had become a tool for sitting, and if sitting were *merely* sitting, then the question of design to relevant purpose would be the criterion of goodness. But what in fact has taken place is not the celebration of an instrumentalistic philosophy of furniture: what we have is the same posture of domination and the same code—so the beast or monster has been replaced by the machine. It is important, then, if the message is to be transmitted, that the chair in question *look* like a machine, polished and functional, powerful and

Vincent van Gogh. *Van Gogh's Chair*
1888—89
Tate Gallery (on loan from
the National Gallery), London

Vincent van Gogh. *Gauguin's Chair*, 1888
Courtesy Vincent van Gogh
Foundation/National Museum
Vincent van Gogh, Amsterdam

swift. To suppose the Barcelona chair or the Wassily chair are simply exemplars of fine design is to display a certain blindness to what it means to sit.

I have one further thought to add to this line of reflection before turning to my next example. In the 1970s and 80s, the chair became funky and droll, as perhaps best seen in certain designs by Michael Graves. Chairs became *fun*. My own historico-political sense suggests that more is happening than this. It is precisely the rejection of domination, of imperialism, turning the chair from slave into playmate, almost plunging away from responsibility: the chair becomes the natural locus for asserting the attitudes of the counterculture. My sense is that the way, then, to tell that we have entered a new political era is to look at the legs we sit on next. Just think what it means when we sit on the floor!

This brings me to my next empty chair, Van Gogh's rush-seated chair painted in late November, 1888, just a month after Gauguin's arrival in Arles, and just a month before the violent quarrel, after which he cut his ear. This was a "honeymoon" period, and the domesticity of the living arrangement of the two painters is emphasized through the fact that Van Gogh does two portraits of their respective chairs, his peasant chair and Gauguin's measurably more elaborate arm chair (it has a carved back, seems to be made of more expensive wood, and is upholstered). Vincent's chair could not be more simple—you can see the knot-hole through the yellow paint. On the seat is his famous pipe—the very pipe he is smoking in his shattering self-portrait with bandaged ear of January, 1889, and with which his identity is clearly and deeply connected. That everything between seat and pipe is withdrawn, that he is not there as solid flesh to separate seat from smoke, suggests the possibility of his body as absent from his image of himself—the kind of attitude we might expect from someone who expresses himself by self-mutilation. The painting is signed "Vincent" on the bulb-box at the left—but it could also be the name of the chair if we read the painting this way: *self-portrait as chair*. And I shall venture a few interpretative remarks against the suggested psychology.

The rush-seated chair is an item of peasant furniture, invented in the late Middle Ages and clearly continuing the connotations of rusticity down to the present era. Until recently, I think, the rush-seated chair would never have found its way into the parlors or social areas of a household with any social pretensions. It belonged in the kitchen, and primarily in the kitchens of country homes. It would symbolize servitude much (I have learned from the architectural historian Christopher Gray) as oak woodwork connoted servants' quarters in Manhattan before World War I; mahogany belonged in the employers' quarters. Only later, when taste turned to the authenticity of natural materials, would the rush seat find its way out of the kitchen (think of where it appears in Chardin). Today, having a rush seat replaced is expensive, but when labor was cheap, as it was in Europe until after World War II, the rush seat must almost have symbolized the worthlessness of labor: the effort exerted on worthless material—straw or pine or oak—made plain that the labor itself went for little. Even so, it seems to me, the rush-seated chair continued to carry a certain authority: the peasant would not, of course, have dominion over beasts and strong enemies, but he would stand something above the vegetable order. In any case, it is a chair for the lowest human order sitting atop the lowest natural order that the rush-seated chair emblemizes.

So, there is a double self-abasement in Van Gogh's portraying himself *as* such a chair. To begin with, to be a chair in the first place is to offer oneself as something to be sat on, which is the first abasement; and then to choose as the chair one is the lowest order of chair in the cosmic scheme everyone in Europe would at that time have accepted, is to execute the other debasement. Even his tobacco pouch and pipe stand higher than he. And this fits completely with the political and religious personality we associate with Vincent: with his identification with the most humble, with his readiness to sacrifice himself, if only symbolically, at the level of conspicuous humility. The chair he painted in November of 1888, in that profound and creative year, is as much a symbol of a certain kind of Christianity as a crucifix. Think of the fact that he signs it with his first name. Only the inferior is so addressed, or the very intimate, either relation being consistent with my reading.

There is a great deal more to talk about in this picture, as in the companion one of Gauguin—which incidentally has a burning candle on the seat where Vincent's has a pipe, leaving room for just the kind of psychoanalytical interpretations I abhor and forbear from developing. But I am anxious to emphasize, as a point about painting, that the enterprise of studying it in terms of colors—of Vincent's chromatic theories, or of the opponent pairings of the color theorist Ewald Hering, which had begun to be of such great interest to the Impressionists and Post-Impressionist painters—that all questions of color contrast, and composition, and spatial invention, ought not blind us to the spiritual meaning of the chair in this painting. It is not that the chair recedes in order to allow the neutral pursuit of optical experiment: if anything there is a war in this painting between two dimensions of Vincent's artistic personality.

Andy Warhol. *Electric Chair*, 1965
Photograph Rudolph Burckhardt;
courtesy Leo Castelli Gallery, New York

My (appropriately) final example of an empty chair is Warhol's 1967 electric chair, which he used in various formats, most strikingly, I think, in the *Lavender Disaster*, where he exploits the familiar television malfunction in which frame after frame presents itself on the screen as we fiddle with the vertical control in an effort to achieve stabilization. The chair serves as little to stabilize society as that control on the television set, and with his usual genius for the selection of images of transcendent power, Warhol confronts us with an image that is absolutely familiar but which corresponds to something we have never seen. Its grainy format contributes to a sense of obscenity. It is a visual intervention into something that has no business being seen or, which perhaps comes to the same thing, we have no business looking at save in the same spirit of prurience that moves us to slow down as we pass accidents on the highway. To use an example in Plato meant to demonstrate weakness of will, the Warhol chair evokes the way we might direct our greedy eyes at a pile of decaying corpses that we know are entitled to the privacy of their own decay under the auspices of decent burial. It is a terrifying image.

The electric chair itself was introduced into capital penology first in New York State in 1888, and though there was controversy as to whether it violated a constitutional prohibition against cruel and unusual punishment, it was put into use in 1890; William Kemmler was the first to sit and never to rise again, in Auburn prison. The chair delivers two thousand volts of electricity, and the theory is that death is instantaneous—much the sort of theory we comfort ourselves with when we plunge lobsters into boiling water, though my thinking is that if we need that kind of reassurance, we have no business using such devices in the first instance.

There are two features of the electric chair that bear mention in the present context. One of them is that it is electric. The electric chair was installed in just the same year, 1888, as Vincent painted the portrait of Gauguin as a chair, and the presence of the candle reminds us that electricity as a means of illumination had not reached Arles in that year. Indeed, the electrification of New York City itself only started, in the form of direct current, in September, 1882. In 1886 only, George Westinghouse demonstrated that it was possible to transmit alternating current across a distance of about four thousand feet. In 1900, there were 356,000 electrical lamps in Paris, a city of two and a half million persons. What is interesting to me in this connection is the thought that electricity should so early be thought of as something that could kill, that the electric chair preceded such things as the electric iron or the electric stove, let alone the electric lamp in the ordinary home. When electricity was introduced in France it seemed simply magical and benign: think of the labor and filth connected with candles and oil and kerosene lamps; electricity was clean, odorless, and would have been cheap but for the taxes. In its first years, it implied luxury, and Eugen Weber's book on *fin de siècle* France reports that it was argued, in that country, when rumor reached it of the electric chair, that electricity *could not kill*. Somehow the perversion of goodness is tangible in the spectacle of the electric chair. So Warhol's image is after all an indictment.

In addition to its being electric, the second fact about the electric chair is that it is a *chair*. What does it not imply about the imagination that saw in electricity a lethal fluid, that it should see in *the chair* the appropriate device to administer death? After all, it could have been an electrical bed, with the victim laid out in the posture of the dead. It could have been an electrical cross. Or the victim could have been required to kneel, as in the guillotine, or under the executioner's axe. Or there could have been an electrical noose, in which the victim, standing on a metallic plate, would close the current transmitted through a cable around his neck. I have no idea of what went through the mind of the inventor. I have no idea of whether what we see in Warhol's picture is the first electric chair or whether there have been "improvements" over time. But my sense is that execution in this manner sufficiently connects with the symbolism of the chair that its being done in the sitting position gives a certain dignity to the death administered. It is as though it were like the last words, the last meal, all those concessions to the prisoner's ceremonial humanity as we send him from our midst: as though giving him a chair to sit in were a form of forgiveness. Meals, farewells, chairs are dense with symbolic transaction, and something of what I have been seeking to convey regarding chairs is made tangible through this terrible image.

The chair, then, is eloquent enough—less eloquent than the nude human body, but eloquent enough—to carry into art a set of powerful human meanings. They may not be universal, but in Western culture, and in large parts of Oriental culture, the meanings are clear enough and part of the shared semiotics of life as a lived system of meaning. That the chair should in recent days have entered art as a medium or a form rather than as subject, that the chair should have become art—subject to a range of surrealist modifications as, say, in the work of Lucas Samaras—strikes me as a sign that a certain barrier has been made visible by being broken. In the act of artistic celebration or artistic aggression (they are perhaps inseparable), we may be trying to liberate ourselves from forms of life that the chair condenses as part of its steady message.

What these forms are and whether we can succeed I leave as an exercise for you; the history of the present will reveal itself only when the present is past and perhaps long past. I was struck by the fact that so many chairs ranged in rows at the Chair Fair at the International Design Center of New York in Long Island City bore the sign "Do Not Sit in This Chair," as if commanding us to reorient ourselves with regard to these objects. To be sure, there were certain others that we would not dare sit in—one covered with white feathers, one made of cereal cartons. None, so far as I could see, was carved in ice, though I have seen, at the Baccarat showroom in Paris, glass chairs that convey the message not to sit without benefit of signs. But institutions and human practices change very slowly, and my sense is that it will be a long time before the chair loses the meanings I have sought to sketch, or drops out completely from the forms of life it anchors. And perhaps when it does so, the chair as art will itself have lost the meaning that comes with treating it with daring and disrespect and fantasy, as in the IDCNY exhibition, which but underscores the extreme potency of the chair as symbol.

On the other hand, the fact that we now show ourselves as having power over the chair, making it funny, or foolish, or amusing, implies, to me at least, that the chair has lost a measure of its own power, and that we in consequence are representing ourselves as having lost a measure of *our* own power. The great chairs of the modern era—the chairs of stunning design—conveyed a confidence in human power as I tried to show before, where in our shining chromium, profoundly industrial sitting pieces, we conveyed our command of the future. We do not have that bold confidence in ourselves that the Barcelona chair or the Brno chair or the Eames chair expresses, and the chair, having ceased to be an emblem of our power, becomes a kind of plaything. The postmodern period of the chair is the postmodern period of human power. So I wonder if the age of the chair is not past because the age of human confidence is past. We simply do not have the kind of control over the forces we need to control to reclaim our dignity. And turning the chair into art has some of the surrender that turning swords into plowshares has. Or, in a more revolutionary way of thinking, the shambling of chairs, the artistic attack on chairs, may be an attack on a concept of power, rank, submission, domination, subservience we feel inconsistent with a more liberal form of life. We could not have found a more potent symbol if these are the social intentions that move the chair from the space of meaning to the space of art.

1 CHRYSLER BUILDING CHAIR

PETER STAMBERG
1986
Wood, nails, glue
18 x 16 x 55″

2 AT&T BUILDING CHAIR

PETER STAMBERG
1986
Wood, nails, glue
20 x 16 x 48″

Note: The first name, appearing in capital letters, indicates the individual or organization which submitted the chair to the exhibition; dimensions, given in inches, are width, depth, and height.

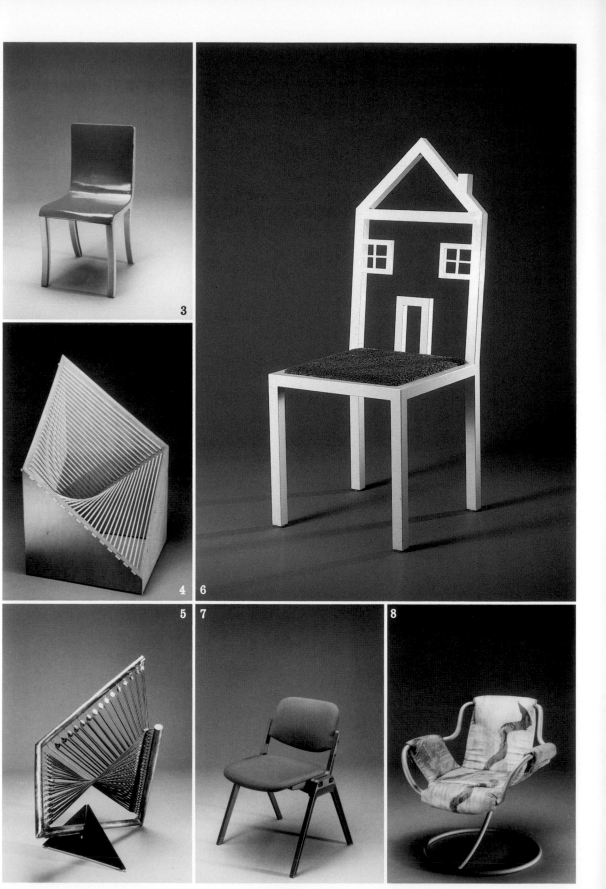

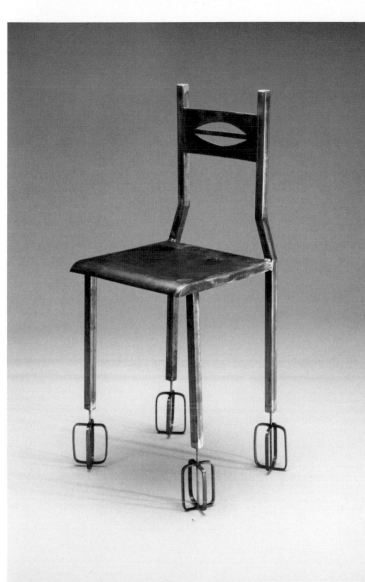

9

13

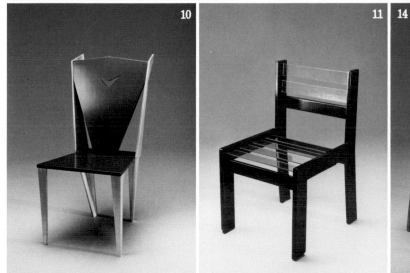

10

11

14

⑨ EGG-BEATER CHAIR

JAMES SCHMIDT
1983
Steel
19 x 16 x 42"

⑩ SIDE CHAIR

GWYN METZ
1983
Aluminum, plywood, metallic
auto body paint
18 x 24 x 38"

⑪ BAUHAUS

HENRY GUTMAN
1985
Baltic birch plywood, Lexan®
19 x 22 x 32"

⑫ TWO-FACED LOVERS

PONI A. BAPTISTÈ
1986
Courtesy of Don Ross and
Schreiber/Cutler Inc., New York
Painted wood, brass, vinyl
18¼ x 15¾ x 38"

⑬ UNNAMED

DONALD CLAY
1986
Pine, poplar
16 x 16 x 48"

⑭ CALITRI

ERMINIO MARRESE
1982
Steam-bent ash
22 x 21 x 32"

15

16 **19** **22**

17 **20** **23**

18 **21** **24**

20 **SEQUENZE**

BFI
1985–6
Designed by Sergio Savarese
Wood, upholstery, metal
27 x 26 x 32"

21 **RIVOLI**

BFC
1986
Designed by Jack Clarke
Hardwood, upholstery
27 x 24 x 33"

22 **UNNAMED**

PETRONE ASSOCIATES
1985
William C. Petrone, designer;
Mark Gould, ass't. designer
Bleached ash
17 x 17 x 36"

23 **SA 147**

SERGIO SAVARESE
1984–5
Metal
17 x 18 x 30"

24 **TERRY DINETTE CHAIR**

ROBERT A. M. STERN ARCHITECTS
1986
Associate in charge: Alan Gerber
Bleached oak, ebony
15 x 15 x 32"

25   BROOKLYN CLUB CHAIR

ROBERT A. M. STERN ARCHITECTS
1986
Associate in charge: Alan Gerber
Vinyl, bird's-eye maple feet
33 x 33 x 31"

26   ROOT CHAIR

JOHN BICKEL
1985
Cherry, walnut, oil finish, wool seat
22 x 22 x 29"

27   GINKO CHAIR

STEPHEN DANIELL
1986
Back, primavera; frame,
painted maple
18 x 18 x 36"

28   CHAIR #8

HANK De RICCO
1983
Chair, cloth, paint
17 x 16 x 36"

29   TRIBUTE TO AFRICA

JOHN BICKEL
1985
Laminated walnut, oil finish
20 x 28 x 40"

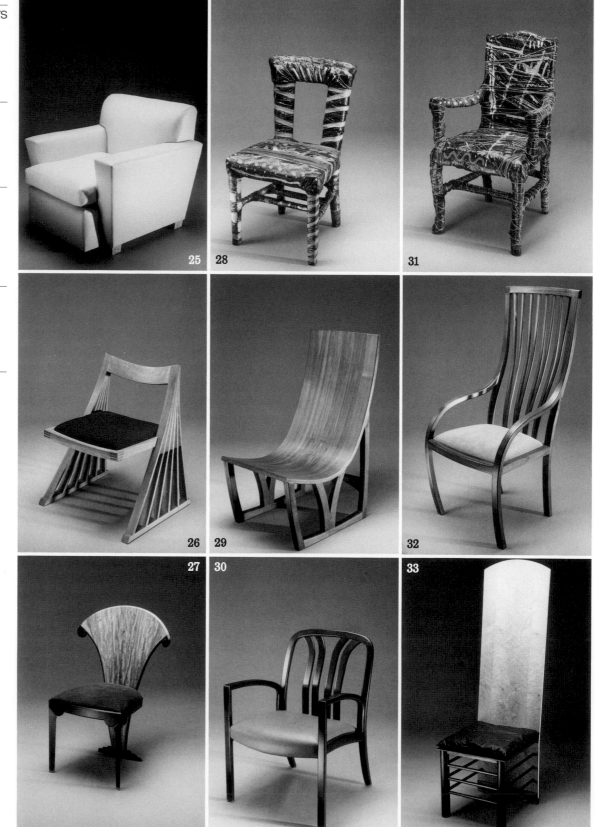

34

30 BRISTOL

THE ALMA COMPANIES
1986
Walnut
23 x 25¾ x 34¾"

31 CHAIR #19

HANK De RICCO
1985
Chair, cloth, paint
16 x 17 x 36"

32 BRANCH BACK CHAIR

JOHN BICKEL
1982
Walnut, oil finish, Ultrasuede® seat
22 x 25 x 45"

33 UNNAMED

PETRONE ASSOCIATES
1985
William C. Petrone, designer;
Mark Gould, ass't. designer
Black stained ash, veneer plywood
18 x 18 x 60"

34 CANOPY CHAIR

JIM MURRAY AND
PAUL VON RINGELHEIM
1986
Maple, aluminum, paint
24 x 20 x 55"

35 DOOR CHAIR

MICHAEL McCOY
1981
Manufactured by Arkitektura
Wood
24 x 24 x 24″

36 FOLDING CHAIR

NEAL MAYER
1986
Birch
19 x 19 x 33″

37 UNNAMED

JIM MURRAY AND
PAUL VON RINGELHEIM
1986
Birch, poplar, paint
20 x 15 x 35″

38 PERSONA

VITRA SEATING, INC.
1984–5
Designed by Mario Bellini
Fiberglass/polyamide shell,
polyurethane/fiberfill cushions,
leather or fabric
22½ x 21¾ x 41¼″

39 IMAGO

VITRA SEATING, INC.
1984/5
Designed by Mario Bellini
Wood, metal, fiberfill-wrapped
polyurethane foam, leather or fabric
29½ x 24 x 45¼″

40 FIGURA

VITRA SEATING, INC.
1984–5
Designed by Mario Bellini
Wood, metal, fiberfill-wrapped
polyurethane foam, leather or fabric
24 x 24 x 40¾″

41 DORSAL MANAGERIAL

KRUEGER
1983
Designed by Emilio Ambasz and
Giancarlo Piretti
Steel, aluminum, extruded
plastic, foam
22¾ x 19 x 37″

38

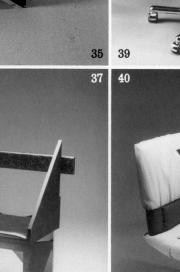

35 39

36 37 40

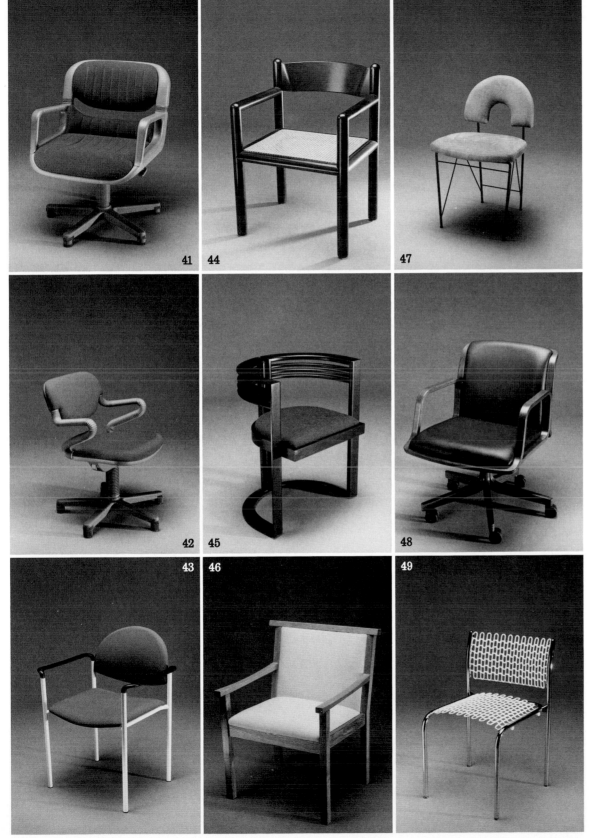

50 ROCKING CHAIR

ROBERT J. CHEHAYL
1980
Maple
31 x 37 x 34"

51 UNNAMED

ELIZABETH KELLEN
1986
Plywood
20 x 27 x 29"

52 UNNAMED

SETH CALLANDER
1986
Birch
18 x 24 x 32"

53 DOLMAS

THONET INDUSTRIES, INC.
1985
Designed by Just Meijer
Laminated beech, polypropylene
20⅝ x 20½ x 30½"

54 UNNAMED

LEE TRENCH
1984
Courtesy of Dr. Donald Wexler
Ash frame, bloodwood,
wool upholstery
44 x 30 x 31"

55 UNNAMED

JOHN DUNNIGAN
1986
Fabric painted in collaboration with
Wahlworks Granadillo, hand-painted
Ultrasuede®, aluminum
28 x 24 x 28"

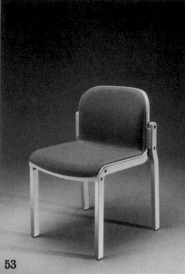

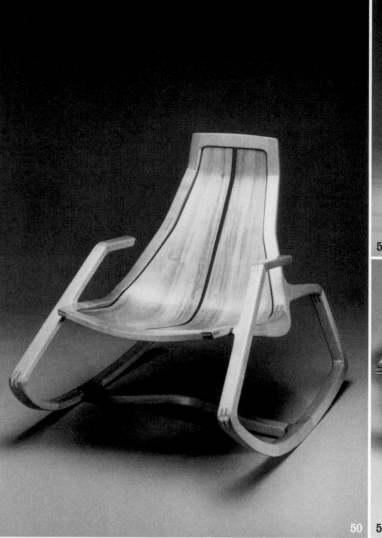

56

57

59

58 60 61

56 SKYSCRAPER CHAIR

HIDETO HORIIKE
1983
Rolling core veneer, quercus wood,
steel pipe
17¾ x 21½ x 53"

57 BROOKHAVEN CHAIR

DAVID N. EBNER
1978
Ebonized oak
18 x 18 x 30"

58 EBNER SWIVEL LOUNGE CHAIR

DAVID N. EBNER
1983
Hand-sprung maple frame,
horsehair, leather, purple heart
28 x 30 x 31"

59 EBNER ROCKER

DAVID N. EBNER
1980
Red oak, cane
26 x 29 x 32"

60 ARMCHAIR

SHIGERU UCHIDA
1986
Courtesy of Gallery 91, New York
Steel
21½ x 21¼ x 31"

61 EASY CHAIR

SHIGERU UCHIDA
1986
Courtesy of Gallery 91, New York
Steel
28 x 24 x 29½"

62 UNNAMED

THOMAS SWIFT
1985
Pin Oak Design
Ebonized walnut, tung oil finish, fabric
20 x 18 x 27"

63 M-2

BRAYTON INTERNATIONAL
COLLECTION
1979
Designed by David de Mayo
Leather, steel, wood, fiber
35 x 35 x 34"

64 CLOU 270

BRAYTON INTERNATIONAL
COLLECTION
1986
Designed by Christian Heimberger
Wood frame, upholstery, Dacron fiber
25½ x 26 x 32¼"

65 FLYING CARPET

CASAFORM
1986
Designed by Simon Desanta; fabric
designed by Dorothy Hafner
Stainless steel tubing, black leather
41 x 41 x 39"

66 ANNA 2046-1

BRAYTON INTERNATIONAL
COLLECTION
1985
Designed by Oswald J. Beck
Beechwood frame, upholstery
22 x 23¼ x 31¼"

67 VANITY FAIR

CASAFORM
1982
Designed by Archivio Frau,
Poltrona Frau S.p.A.
Beechwood, steel, jute, leather,
horsehair, down feathers
30 x 37 x 37"

62

63

65

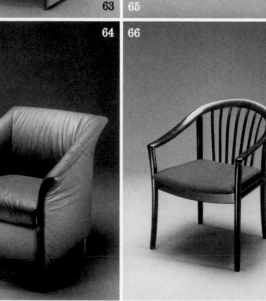

64

66

67

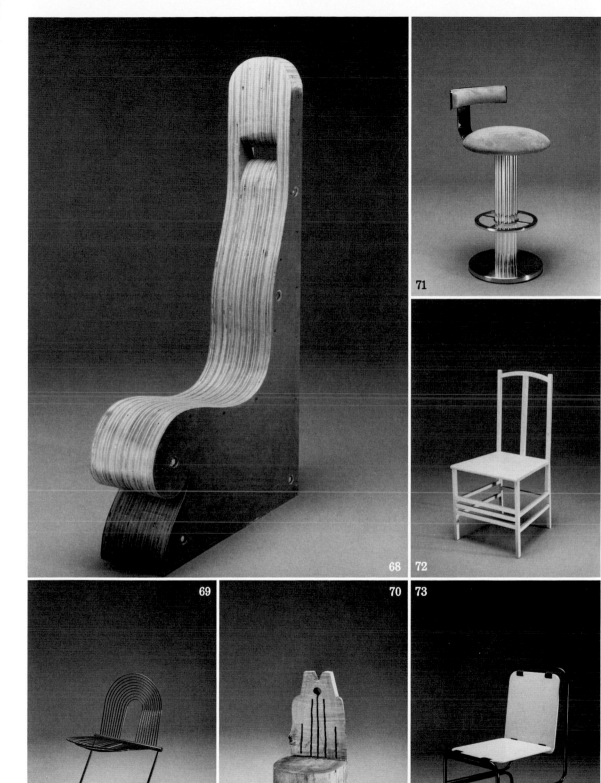

68 OY X LL CHAIR
DAVID SELLERS
1986
Sellers & Company, Architects
Laminated Baltic birch plywood
8 x 26 x 42″

69 SWING
CASAFORM
1984
Designed by Herbert and Jutta Ohl
Flexible steel
18 x 22 x 31″

70 60-SECOND CHAIR:
ONE TREE TRUNK AND
CHAIN SAW
DAVID SELLERS
1981
Sellers & Company, Architects
Wood
16 x 16 x 31″

71 EXCALIBUR
DESIGNS FOR LEISURE, INC.
1980
Metal
18 x 18 x 39″

72 CAFÉ CHAIR
JOHN LONCZAK
1981–2
Plywood
16½ x 17¼ x 36½″

73 CORREA
DAVID PERRY
1984
Courtesy Functional Art Gallery
Steel, painted wood
17 x 19½ x 43″

74 HIGHLAND WOODWORKS CHAIR

BRUCE MacPHAIL
1985
Highland Woodworks
Cherry, maple, leather
18 x 18 x 34"

75 THE MEIER CHAIR

RICHARD MEIER
1982
Manufactured by Knoll International
Laminated hard maple veneers,
black lacquer–urethane finish
21 x 20 x 27½"

76 DE WITT CHAIR

DAVID EDWARD, LTD.
1986
Designed by P. de Witt
Wood, foam, fabric
20½ x 19¾ x 30¼"

77 UNNAMED

JIM ABBOTT
1986
Aluminum
24 x 24 x 36"

78 THRONE

PAMELA SLASS
1985
Mahogany, plywood, paint, leather
38 x 20 x 84"

79 STATESMAN'S ARMCHAIR

LARSEN FURNITURE
1985
Designed by Ernst Dettinger
European beech
22 x 25 x 36¼"

80 UNNAMED

CHRISTOPHER FARLEY
1984
Wood and rubber
23⅛ x 23 x 49"

81 CROWN

SHEILA BERKLEY
1986
Fiberglass laminate, aluminum,
glass, paint
24 x 33 x 36"

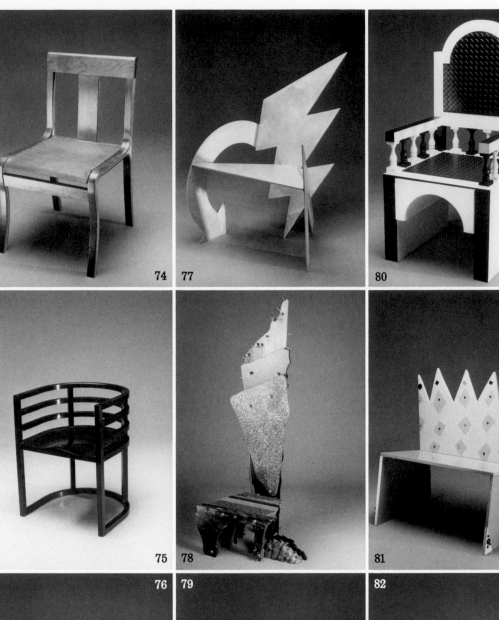

74 77 80

75 78 81

76 79 82

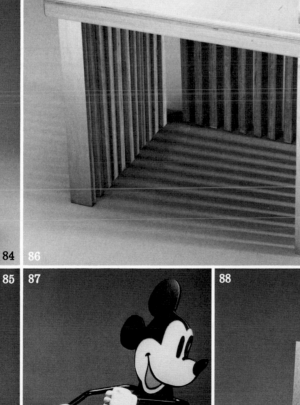

82 AUTUMN SITE CHAIR

AUDREY HEMENWAY
1986
Frescoed ferrocement
19 x 19½ x 33½"

83 PLANETARIUM CHAIR

INDUSTRIAS FIGUERAS, S.A.
1986
Designed by Salvador Perez Arroyo
for Madrid Planetarium
Steel, molded foam, inner springs
25⅝ x 30½ x 40½"

84 EXETER CHAIR

WARREN S. FENZI
1985
Honduras mahogany,
ebony detailing, fabric
21 x 23 x 42"

85 CRATER LAKE CHAIR

WARREN S. FENZI
1981
Maple, lacquer, leather
28 x 25 x 28"

86 UNTITLED [PROTOTYPE]

JULIANNE JONES
1983
Birch plywood and pine
24½ x 21 x 28"

87 MOUSKACHAIR

CATHERINE WALSH
1984
Plywood, metal tubing, polyfoam
23 x 27 x 60"

88 CONSTANTIN CHAIR

CONSTANTIN BOYM
1986
Black lacquered wood, recomposed
wood veneers
21 x 17 x 32"

89 QUINTA™/TIGE

STEVEN K. LEVINE
1986
The Quinta™ Collection
(patents pending, © 1986 SKL)
Steel tubing, plywood, fabric
24 x 25 x 32"

90 QUINTA™/SANDER

STEVEN K. LEVINE
1986
The Quinta™ Collection
(patents pending, © 1986 SKL)
Steel tubing, plywood, fabric
24 x 25 x 32"

91 QUINTA™/SIDNEY

STEVEN K. LEVINE
1986
The Quinta™ Collection
(patents pending, © 1986 SKL)
Steel tubing, plywood, fabric
24 x 25 x 32"

92 SET PIECE FROM 'SOMBRAS DE AGUA'

ALAN GLOVSKY
1986
Wood, steel, paint
17 x 18 x 77"

93 VENETIAN LOUNGE

BONAVENTURE FURNITURE
INDUSTRIES, LTD.
1983
Designed by Stanley Jay Friedman
Wood frame, leather
28½ x 37 x 28½"

94 SCHOLARIS CHAIR

BONAVENTURE FURNITURE
INDUSTRIES, LTD.
1984
Designed by Stanley Jay Friedman
Wood frame, leather
23½ x 24½ x 31½"

95 ANDOVER

STENDIG INTERNATIONAL, INC.
1984
Designed by Davis Allen/SOM
Beech, foam, upholstery
22 x 22½ x 36"

96 RIBBON

STENDIG INTERNATIONAL, INC.
1986
Designed by Calvin Morgan
Ash, foam, upholstery
24½ x 21½ x 31"

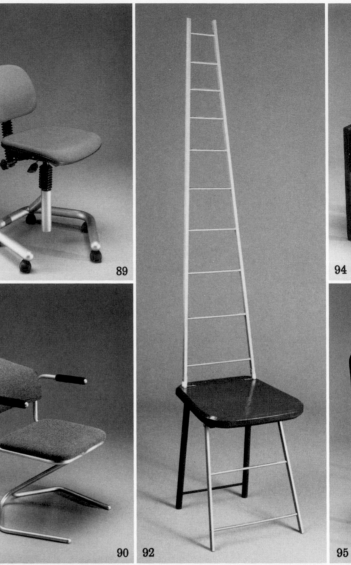

89

90 92

91 93

94

95

96

97   100   103

98   101   104

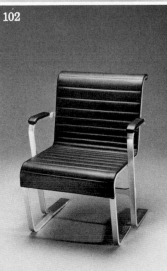

99   102   105

98 TELEPHONE TABLE

RINALDO FRATTOLILLO
1977
Lacquer over veneer
30 x 26 x 30"

99 WALTER

WALTER/BOOTH DESIGN
1986
Fabricated by General Specialties
Steel, rubber
18 x 34 x 20"

100 THRONES

RICHARD MARENCIC
1985
Plywood, plastic laminate
24 x 24 x 72"

101 LAUREN CHAIR

CADSANA
1986
Designed by Richard Schultz
Plywood, aluminum, foam, fabric
23½ x 19 x 34"

102 BREUER SIDE CHAIR

CADSANA
1986
Newly adapted from a
Marcel Breuer design
Polished aluminum extrusion, wood
20 x 17½ x 32¾"

103 GINA

STENDIG INTERNATIONAL, INC.
1981
Designed by Bernd Makulik
Beech, foam, upholstery
22¾ x 22 x 33"

104 SORO CHAIR

CADSANA
1983
Designed by Francesco Soro
Steel rod, harness leather
19¾ x 19¾ x 29⅞"

105 FM 60/61/62

UMS-PASTOE
1981
Designed by Radboud van Beekum
Steel tubing, leather, wood, canvas
24 x 28 x 15¼"

106 TON TON

KAZUO KAWASAKI
1984
Courtesy Gallery 91; affiliated
w/Maruichi Sailing, Japan
Metal piping and foamed
polyurethane with nylon fabric
31½ x 31½ x 18"

107 BARTO 3945

M. RICHARD SCHULTZ
1984
Designed by M. Richard Schultz for
Domore Corporation
PVC, cast and corrugated steel,
leather upholstery
25½ x 18 x 36"

108 LUCA

ANDREA PONSI
1986
Copper tubing, leather, foam
18 x 23 x 42"

109 STRADA LOUNGE 2310

ROBERT De FUCCIO
1985
Designed by Robert De Fuccio for
Domore Corporation
Beech bentwood, leather
28⅜ x 29⁹⁄₁₆ x 28"

110 UNNAMED

CHARLES F. LOWREY
1982
Steel, sheet metal
21¼ x 22½ x 31½"

111 LORENZO ONE

LLOYD BELL, FASID
1986
Polished stainless steel
15½ x 16 x 22"

106

107   109

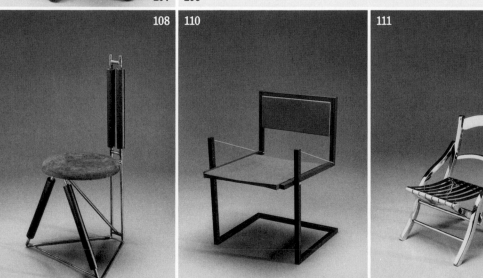

108   110   111

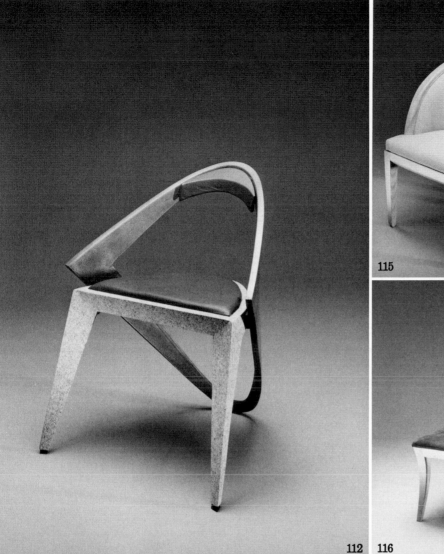

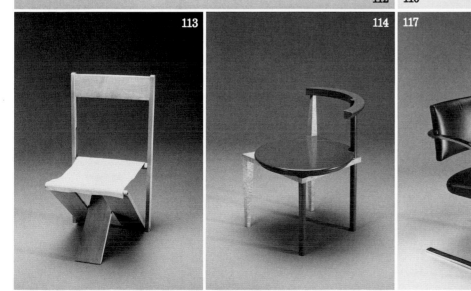

112 CHEVRON

MICHAEL ROY MENSCH
1983
Wood, fabric, steel hardware, foam
28 x 32 x 36"

113 FOLDING CHAIR

STEPHEN DAYTON
1982
Maple, canvas
17 x 17 x 36"

114 META-CHAIR

GREGORY EITELMAN
1986
Veneer, paint
20 x 18 x 27"

115 NANCY CHAIR

STANLEY FELDERMAN
1984
Leason Pomeroy Felderman
Associates
Ash frame, Chamosault fabric
24 x 24 x 32¾"

116 BOULLÉE CHAIR

JACK MILLARD
1985
Available through Dennis Miller
Associates, New York
Maple
18 x 20 x 32"

117 MASCHERONI CHAIR

BRUETON INDUSTRIES, INC.
1984
Designed by Mark Mascheroni
Stainless steel
22 x 23½ x 31"

118 UNNAMED

CRISTINA NIETO
1986
Steel
19 x 15 x 60″

119 DUFFY

BRUETON INDUSTRIES, INC.
1978
Designed by John Duffy
Stainless steel, wood,
springs, polyfoam
22¼ x 25½ x 31½″

120 MARCO

BRUETON INDUSTRIES, INC.
1984
Designed by Mark Goldberg
Stainless steel tubing, metal
armature, webbing, foam
22 x 22 x 31½″

121 HENRY FORD

DENNIS CONNORS
1985
Steel
36 x 36 x 96″

122 DINING CHAIR

GWEN-LIN GOO
1981–2
Courtesy of Agnes Gund
Stainless steel, woven stainless
steel
18½ x 21½ x 45½″

123 EMPIRE LOUNGE

BRUETON INDUSTRIES, INC.
1984
Designed by Stanley Jay Friedman
Stainless steel, upholstery
21 x 21 x 28″

118

121

122

119 120

123

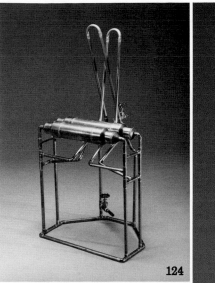

124

125

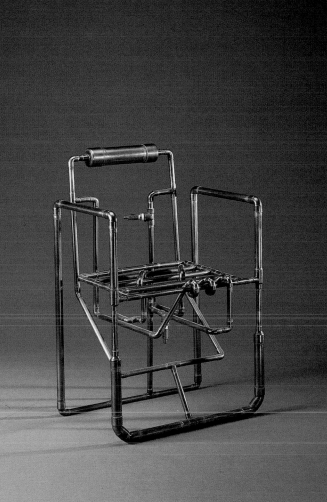

127

126

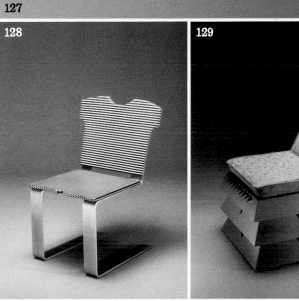

128

129

133

130

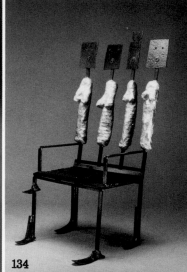

134

131

132

135

136

133 **UNNAMED**

JAMES HUTCHINSON
1985
Cherry
16 x 14 x 42″

134 **WOMB CHAIR**

MICHAEL RABIN
1986
Steel, cast iron, plaster, gold leaf
28¼ x 25½ x 59″

135 **LIBERTY**

BRUETON INDUSTRIES, INC.
1985
Designed by Stanley Jay Friedman
Hardwood, polyfoam
26 x 26 x 31″

136 **HUMMING**

SINYA OKAYAMA
1984
Courtesy of Gallery 91, New York
Steel, plastic coating, fabric
22½ x 21½ x 32½″

137 UNNAMED

DONALD KRAWCZYK
1986
Ash, milk paint, cotton fabric
19 x 20½ x 36½"

138 PADIAK ROCKER

SCOTT PADIAK
1986
Nylon, steel, wood, fiberglass,
rubber
24½ x 39 x 34"

139 VERTEBRA
OPERATIONAL

EMILIO AMBASZ
1977
Polypropylene shell, self-skinned
steel base, fabric or leather
19¼ x 23 x 36½"

140 SWIVEL

NINA YANKOWITZ
1986
Courtesy of Art et Industrie,
New York
© 1986 Nina Yankowitz
Ceramic tile, marble, wood
18½ x 17 x 33½"

141 LUMB-R

EMILIO AMBASZ
1983
Plywood, self-skinned steel base
21 x 19 x 31"

142 UNNAMED

JACK MANDEL
1986
Jackhammer Industrial, Inc.
Ash, aluminum, Kevlar
12 x 18 x 36"

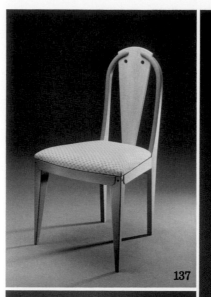

137

138

140

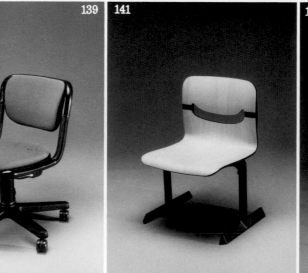

139

141 142

143

144

148

145

146

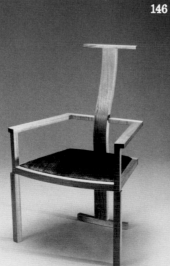

149

143 PEACOCK CHAIR

CONSTANTIN BOYM
1985
Aluminum tubing, wood, fabric
20 x 18 x 37"

144 PEAHEN CHAIR

CONSTANTIN BOYM
1986
Aluminum tubing, wood, fabric
12 x 18 x 30"

145 UNNAMED

MITCHELL ACKERMAN
1977
(Patented design)
Birch, maple, metal
25 x 18 x 34"

146 TRIPOD CHAIR

STEPHEN R. LaDREW
1986
Wood (muiracatiara), upholstery
23 x 21 x 39"

147 ARMCHAIR

STEPHEN R. LaDREW
1983
Wood (padauk), upholstery
23 x 21 x 39"

148 OSCAR STACKING ARMCHAIR

ICF INC.
1983
Designed by Oscar Tusquets
Steel, molded foam-covered
fiberglass, leather armrests
21⅝ x 23⅝ x 32¾"

149 DR. SONDERBAR

ICF INC.
1982
Designed by Philippe Starck
Steel tubing, perforated steel
35½ x 18½ x 24¾"

150 McCHAIR

ADAM St. JOHN
1985
Birch, alkyd enamel
22 x 24 x 35″

151 SECONDA ARMCHAIR

ICF INC.
1982
Designed by Mario Botta
Steel tubing, perforated steel,
polyurethane
20½ x 22¾ x 28¼″

152 CHAIR

J. B. BLUNK
1984
Courtesy of Snyderman Gallery,
Philadelphia
Redwood
29 x 26 x 49″

153 CAIN CHAIR

ROBERT A. ERICKSON
1986
Courtesy of Snyderman Gallery,
Philadelphia
Madrone, rosewood, leather
20 x 17 x 37″

154 FLOATING BACK ROCKER

ROBERT A. ERICKSON
1986
© 1986 Robert A. Erickson
California black oak
40 x 24 x 46″

155 MINOANESQUE CHAIR

DAVID VAN NOSTRAND
1986
Courtesy of Snyderman Gallery,
Philadelphia
Black walnut
17 x 22 x 36″

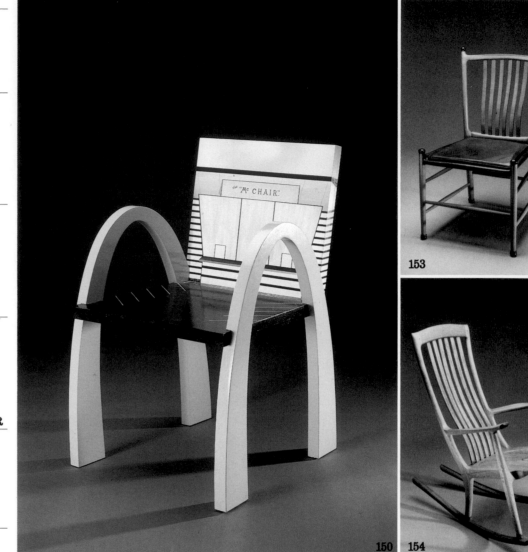

153

150 154

151   152   155

156

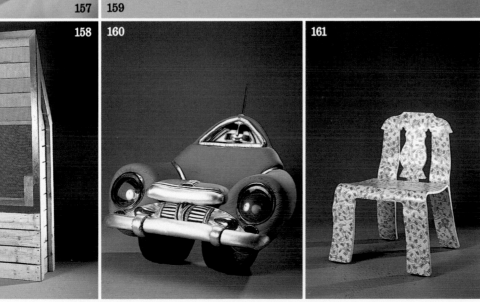

157 159

158 160 161

156 THE DERECKTOR CHAIR

DERECKTOR FURNITURE
1986
Honduras mahogany, brass
27½ x 25 x 33½"

157 AILERON

BIDDINGER/TODD
1986
Lacquered aluminum, leather
31 x 33 x 28"

158 THE BLIND MAN'S
HOUSE-CHAIR

WENDA HABENICHT
1986
Wood, wire screen
28 x 16¾ x 85¼"

159 TSU CHAIR

BRUETON INDUSTRIES, INC.
1980
Designed by Stanley Jay Friedman
Mahogany, polyfoam, stainless
steel or bronze leg sabots
25¼ x 22½ x 33½"

160 MERYLMOBILE

GARY SCHATMEYER
1980
Leather over foam and wood
55 x 60 x 52"

161 EMPIRE CHAIR

ROBERT VENTURI and
DENISE SCOTT BROWN
1984
Manufactured by Knoll International
Bentwood laminations,
laminate or wood veneer face
24¼ x 23⅜ x 32½"

162 UNNAMED

DOUGLAS GERALD FITCH
1986
Polyurethane foam, fiberglass,
upholstery
48 x 32 x 40″

163 SWAN

THOM McHUGH, ARCHITECT
1980
Wood base, metal frame,
stretch fabric
36 x 36 x 34″

164 SHAKER HOUSE CHAIR

FERNANDO MARTINEZ
1986
Aluminum, quilted cotton duck fabric
18 x 18 x 48″

165 SHERATON CHAIR

ROBERT VENTURI and
DENISE SCOTT BROWN
1984
Manufactured by Knoll International
Bentwood laminations,
laminate or wood veneer face
23⅛ x 23⅞ x 33½″

162

162

163

164

165

166

167

168

169

166 UNNAMED

DOUGLAS GERALD FITCH
1986
Polyurethane foam, fiberglass
27 x 23 x 34″

167 UNNAMED

DOUGLAS GERALD FITCH
1986
Polyurethane foam, fiberglass
28 x 22 x 34″

168 CHIPPENDALE CHAIR

ROBERT VENTURI and
DENISE SCOTT BROWN
1984
Manufactured by Knoll International
Bentwood laminations,
laminate or veneer face
25½ x 23¼ x 37⅜″

169 ADIRONDACK ATTACK

BARRY HOLDEN
1986
Wood, neon
36 x 31 x 38″

170 DINING CHAIR

MARK SFIRRI
1978
Maple, shedua
23 x 21 x 31"

171 MESON CHAIR

FORM AND COLOR, INC.
1986
Ash, ebony
15 x 17 x 38"

172 PEELED MAPLE

DANIEL MACK
1985
Daniel Mack Rustic Furnishings
Maple
18 x 20 x 42"

173 LORRY CHAIR

THOMAS LEAR GRACE
1984
Grace Designs
Bent plywood, maple, black paint
16 x 20 x 36"

170

171 173

172 174

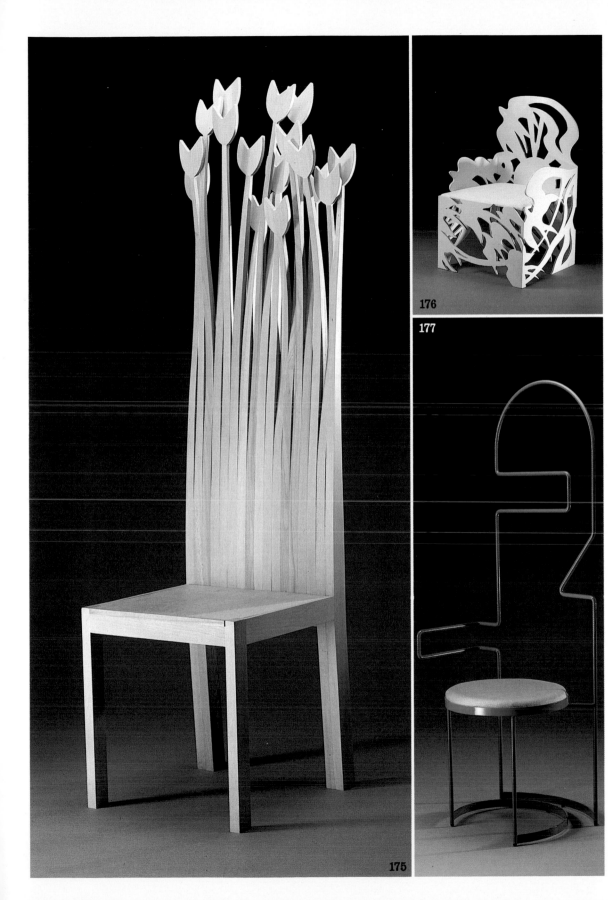

175

176

177

176
177

174	**LOVE SEAT**

JENNIFER SAGE
1986
Mixed media
36 x 18 x 34″

175	**EASTER (TULIP CHAIR)**

LESLIE GOODCHILD
1986
Beech
18¾ x 17 x 65″

176	**GOOD MORNING**

VICTOR AMADOR
1985
Painted plywood
24 x 22 x 40″

177	**MAX**

JOEL A. SMITH
1986
½″ steel wire, foam, fabric,
nylon, Imron paint
17 x 17 x 54¾″

178 THE POOL CHAIR

STEVEN HOLT and TUCKER
VIEMEISTER with LISA KROHN
1986
Steel tubing, acrylic,
ceramic tile, pool accessories
30 x 30 x 36"

179 POMPEIIAN LOUNGE

BONAVENTURE FURNITURE
INDUSTRIES, LTD.
1983
Designed by Stanley Jay Friedman
Wood frame, leather
28 x 40 x 30"

180 WISH YOU WERE HERE

WILLIAM J. SLOANE
1986
Aluminum, aramith, dyed and
hand-printed rayon
27 x 31 x 32"

181 ARTIFORT HELLO THERE

KRUEGER INTERNATIONAL
1980
Designed by Jeremy Harvey
Die-cast aluminum, PVC
15 x 16½ x 29½"

182 REGENCY LOUNGE

BONAVENTURE FURNITURE
INDUSTRIES, LTD.
1983
Designed by Stanley Jay Friedman
Wood frame, leather
28 x 41 x 25"

178

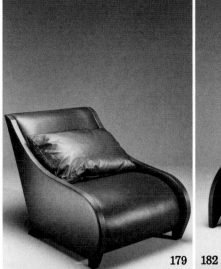

179 182

185

180 183

186

181

184

187

191

188

192

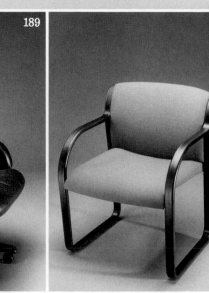

189

190

193

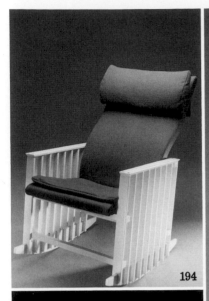

194

195

197

196

198

199

194 ROCKING CHAIR

JOHN RIZZI
1985
Plywood, Imron paint
24 x 38 x 28"

195 BOLERO

RONALD BRICKE
1986
Ronald Bricke & Associates
Plywood, rubberized hair,
down, feathers, springs
23 x 31½ x 30"

196 DORIC CHAIR

DAVID P. LEIGHLY
1986
Birch, suede, leather
22½ x 22½ x 27"

197 DIFFERENCE OF OPINION (NOT A LOVE SEAT)

MICHAEL LALICKI
1986
Wood, paint, plastic
24 x 33 x 66"

198 VERONDA

INTERNA DESIGNS
1978
Designed by George Veronda
Steel
20½ x 22 x 30½"

199 RIB CHAIR

HENRY OLKO
1977
Willow & Reed, Inc.
Manau rattan
40 x 38 x 28"

200 ADRIENNE

JAMES D'AURIA ASSOCIATES
ARCHITECTS
1986
Aluminum, Dacron/foam fill,
linen/silk upholstery
24 x 30 x 38"

201 1255 CLUB CHAIR

HENRY OLKO
1983
Willow & Reed, Inc.
Ash frame, hand-wrapped
with split rattan
24½ x 24 x 29"

202 CHAIR 2

SEPPO SIIMES
1986
Wood, plastic laminate
18 x 24 x 48"

203 LE FAUTEUIL

STEPHEN CARTER
1979
Polished chrome, leather
22½ x 22½ x 31½"

204 ARMCHAIR

DAVID G. FLATT
1978
Laminated walnut
26 x 24 x 37"

205 SIDE CHAIR

DAVID G. FLATT
1976
Laminated walnut
24 x 22 x 39"

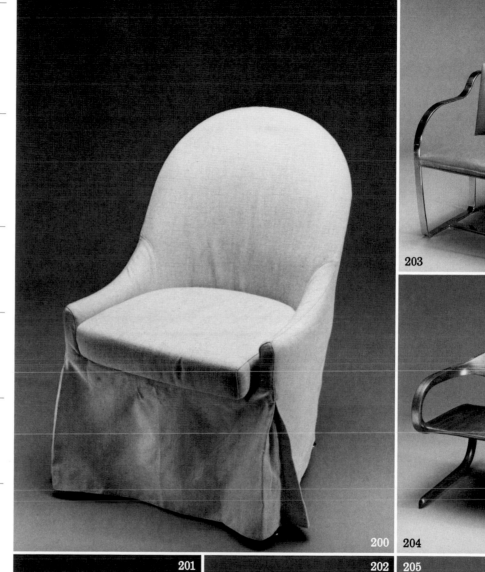

200

203

204

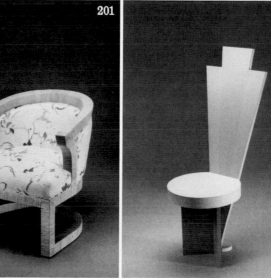

201

202

205

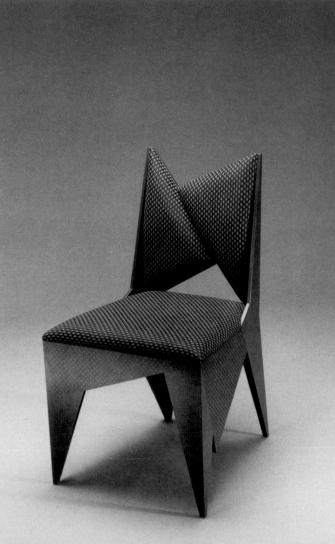

206 210

209

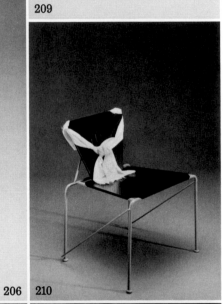

207

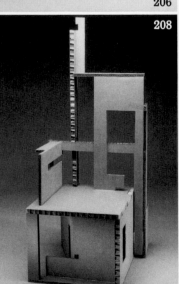

208

211

212 "A THRONE FOR THE DISHEVELED" VALET

PAUL GURDA
1985
Poplar dowels, stained ash
seat/trim, steel hinges
28 x 28 x 54" folded;
13 x 56 x 54" extended

213 GREEK STOOL

PAUL GURDA
1986
Curly maple (frame, legs);
mahogany (seat)
14 x 14 x 14"

214 MORGAN DECK CHAIR

VOORSANGER & MILLS
ASSOCIATES ARCHITECTS
1983
Stained redwood
24 x 28 x 40"

215 ROCK 'N ROLL

GREGG FLEISHMAN
1984
Courtesy of Functional Art Gallery,
Los Angeles
Finnish birch plywood
23½ x 95½ x ⅝" thick

215

216

212

213

214

217

218

219 UNNAMED

STEPHEN SCHERMEYER
1981
Steel rods and seat
24 x 20 x 29″

220 SMOKING CLUB CHAIR

ANGUS J. BRUCE
1980
Mahogany and plastic laminate
44 x 30 x 30″

221 SPRING

TERJE HOPE
1984
Available through Westnofa, Chicago
Laminated birch
19½ x 19½ x 39¼″

222 TIKA CHAIR

DENIS R. DAMBREVILLE
1986
Metal, acajou wood
17 x 17 x 36″

225

223   **UNNAMED**

PAMELA McCORMICK
1986
Wood
72 x 36 x 72″ (foot print 14 x 14″)

224   **100/325**

KINETICS
1986
Designed by Salmon Hamilton
Designs
1¼″ tubular steel, steel seat,
molded foam, upholstery
23½ x 29 x 43″

225   **700/100**

KINETICS
Revised 1976
Designed by Salmon Hamilton
Designs
1½″ tubular steel, spun steel seat
16 x 16 x 28″

226 100/310

KINETICS
1986
Designed by Salmon Hamilton
Designs
1¼" tubular steel, structured foam
seat/back
21½ x 22 x 29½"

227 NEOCHAIR

WILLIAM HENDRICK
1984
Manufactured by Mueller Furniture
Corporation
Laminated maple, walnut veneer,
tubular steel, webbing, foam
23½ x 25 x 35¾"

228 BØRSEN HIGH-BACK

MUELLER FURNITURE
CORPORATION
1986
Designed by Takashi Okamura and
Erik Marquardsen
Leather upholstery over tubular steel
30½ x 36 x 39½"

229 UNNAMED

CARSON AHLMAN
1986
Finished plywood
30 x 29 x 39"

230 BLACK FOREST

JERRY KOTT
1986
Wood, leather
19 x 15½ x 43"

231 RUSTIC WRIGHT

DANIEL MACK
1986
Daniel Mack Rustic Furnishings
Hand-split pin oak
20 x 24 x 46"

226

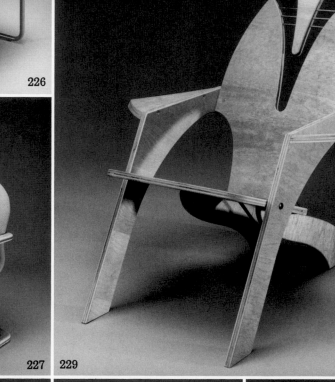

227   229

228

230

231

232

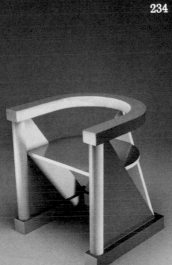

235

236

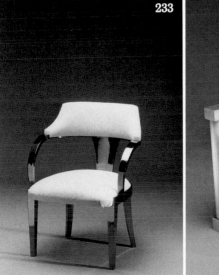

233

234

237

232 CHILD'S ROCKER

MITCH RYERSON
1986
Maple, cherry, clothespins,
washboard, soapbox labels
16 x 14 x 24"

233 EVANS CHAIR

CAROLE GRATALE, INC.
1935; never reproduced
Designed by David L. Evans
Gunmetal frame, leather upholstery
24 x 24 x 33"

234 SARALEE CHAIR

DANIEL RIVAS
1982
Painted plywood
22½ x 23 x 30"

235 PROMETHEUS CHAIR

JACK MILLARD
1983
Available through Dennis Miller
Associates, New York
Maple, leather
23½ x 20½ x 30"

236 109 STOOL

RAUL ROSAS, ARCHITECT
1979
Sugar pine, maple
16 x 14 x 26"

237 LA LUNA

BIJAN SAFAVI
1983
Wood, leather
15 x 15 x 50"

STEPHENS OFFICE SEATING

WILLIAM STEPHENS
1982
Manufactured by Knoll International
Cast aluminum, plywood,
molded foam
Maximum 30½ x 27½ x 37½"

238

239

239 **NEVELE CHAIR**

ALAN BUCHSBAUM/
MARC LITALIEN
1986
Wood frame, foam/Dacron fill, wool
47 x 43 x 35"

240 **RUDI**

ROSS MacTAGGART
1984
Mahogany plywood, brass grille
18 x 27 x 72"

241 **STEEL CIRCLE CHAIR**

ALISON SLON
1986
Steel
26 x 22 x 54"

242 **ROCKING CHAIR**

DAVID P. BARRESI
1979
Oil-finished white ash, leather
36 x 54 x 42"

243 **I HAIGH IT, I HAIGH
EVERYTHING ABOUT IT**

THOMAS HUCKER
1985
Gray lacquered plywood,
wenge wood base
44 x 14 x 30"

244 **STAINED GLASS**

FRANCISCO CABRAL
1986
Steel, wood, glass
36 x 36 x 128"

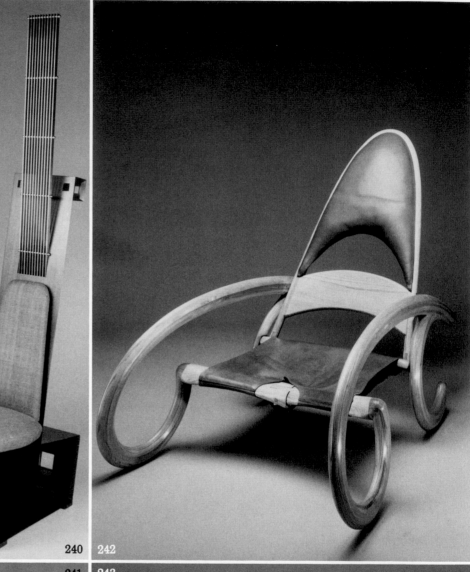

240

242

241

243

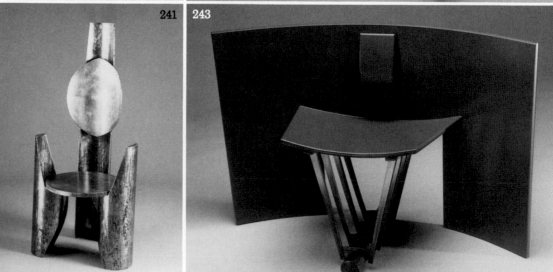

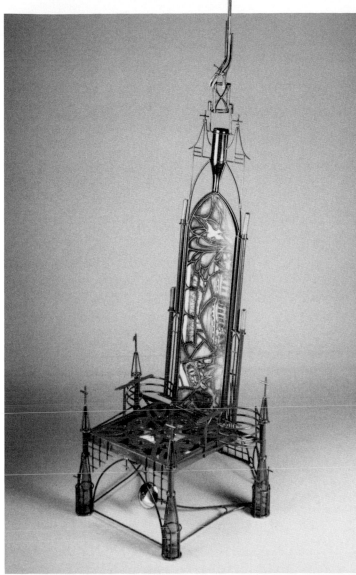

244

247

248

245

246   **249**

245 STACKING CHAIR

CURTIS ERPELDING
1982
Bent laminated maple
19 x 19 x 32"

246 DIFFRIENT MANAGEMENT CHAIR

NIELS DIFFRIENT
1980
14 gauge stamped steel shell;
lever-activated height adjust
27 x 25⅜ x 32"

247 DIFFRIENT EXECUTIVE CHAIR

NIELS DIFFRIENT
1980
Molded plywood back frame,
polymer diaphragm seat
26⅜ x 26¼ x 38¼"

248 DIFFRIENT SIDE CHAIR

NIELS DIFFRIENT
1985
14 gauge steel frame and
stamped steel seat shell
24⅞ x 25¾ x 32¼"

249 FINE FORM ARMCHAIR

GORDON INTERNATIONAL
1985
Designed by Ernest W. Beranek
Wood, metal trim
21¼ x 23¼ x 41¾"

250 | COLUMN/GRID CHAIR

BUMPZOID
(B. BENEDICT/C. PUCCI)
1981
Ash
24 x 24 x 33½"

251 | CHAIR WITH A PAST

BARBARA GOODSTEIN
1986
Courtesy of Bowery Gallery,
New York
Hydrocal plaster, wood, cotton,
jute and fiberglass cloth
24 x 34 x 31"

252 | PROVIDENCE PARTNERSHIP CHAIR

PROVIDENCE PARTNERSHIP
1985
Mahogany, wool/silk upholstery
16 x 16 x 42"

253 | DINING SIDE CHAIR

DAVID L. HUTCHINSON
1984
Lacquered wood, stainless steel,
fabric
19 x 21 x 39"

254 | LIBRARY CHAIR WITH OTTOMAN

DAVID L. HUTCHINSON
1985
Lacquered wood, fabric upholstery
32 x 30 x 32"

250   252   253

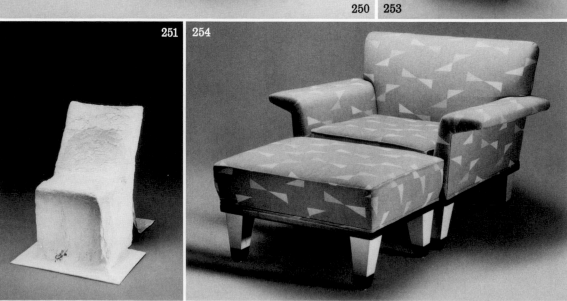

251   254

255

256

258

257

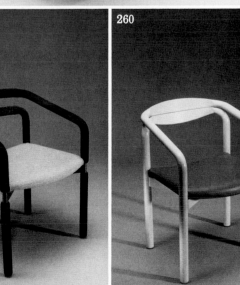

259

260

255 **ROSE CHAIR**

FURNITURE OF THE TWENTIETH
CENTURY
1985
Designed by Michael Formica
Wrought iron with clear oil finish
15½ x 15½ x 33½"

256 **MANHATTAN CHAIR**

CHARLES McMURRAY DESIGNS
1985
Cherry wood
21¼ x 22¾ x 32"

257 **PEGASUS CHAIR**

D.V. JOHNSON
1985
Cherry inlaid with brass and
stainless steel
21 x 24 x 40"

258 **PLANE ROCKER # 1
[PROTOTYPE]**

ROBERT A. COHEN with
RICHARD LOMUTO and
PETER LYNCH
1986
Bent ⅛" laminated poplar
23½ x 35½ x 50½

259 **617 RUBBER CHAIR**

METROPOLITAN FURNITURE
CORP.
1983
Designed by Brian Kane
Steel frame, polypropylene
straps, rubber tubing
22 x 22 x 30"

260 **680 WOOD CHAIR**

METROPOLITAN FURNITURE
CORP.
1986
Designed by Brian Kane
Laminated beech veneers,
polyurethane foam
22 x 23 x 30"

261 HOMAGE TO AMERICAN DREAM

STOMU MIYAZAKI
1985
Painted wood, aluminum,
artificial grass
24 x 20 x 33"

262 TONIETTA

FURNITURE OF THE TWENTIETH
CENTURY
1985
Designed by Enzo Mari
Aluminum alloy, cowhide
15¼ x 18½ x 33"

263 CAFÉ COSTES

FURNITURE OF THE TWENTIETH
CENTURY
1984
Designed by Philippe Starck
Iron tubing, bent plywood,
stuffed leather cushion
19 x 22 x 31"

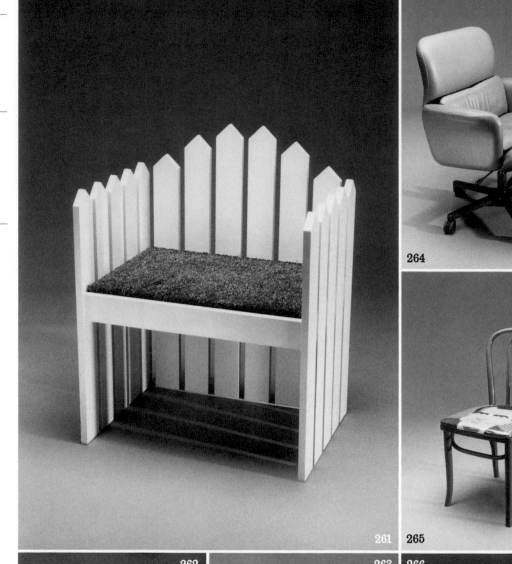

261

264

265

262

263

266

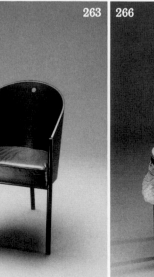

264 **633 MONTARA EXECUTIVE CHAIR**

METROPOLITAN FURNITURE
CORP.
1986
Designed by Brian Kane
Fiberglass shell, polyurethane foam,
cast aluminum
24½ x 27½ x 35"

265 **NIXON CHAIR**

MARGARET CUSACK
1976
Wood, fabric, thread, clear vinyl
16 x 16 x 36"

266 **UNNAMED**

RICHELMO BOTTINO
1986
Ebonized ash, copper cloth, silver
16 x 18 x 32"

267 **HIGH-BACK SIDE CHAIR**

MARC NUGENT
1985
Cherry frame, laminated cherry
and hardwood seat
16 x 21 x 52¾"

267

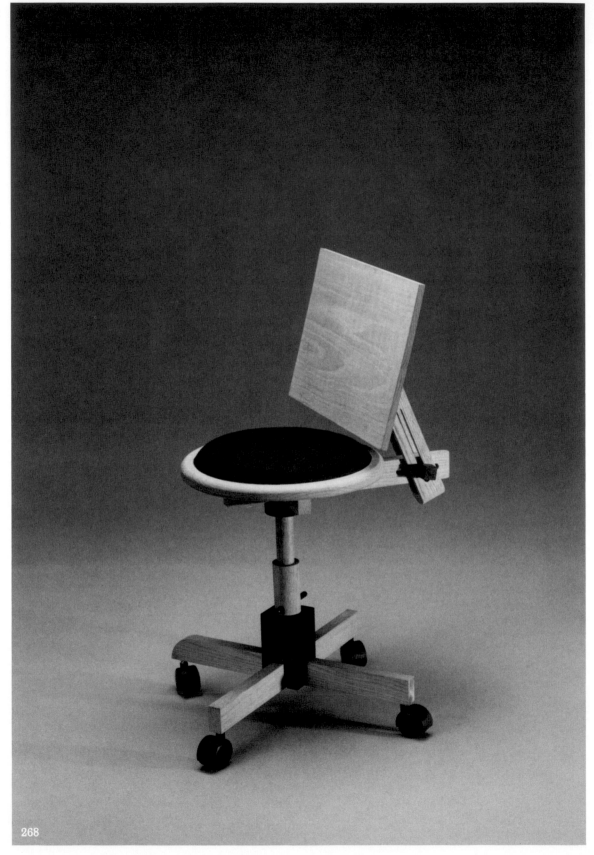

268 DE STOJL

MARK GOULD, DAVID ROTH &
MICHAEL PETRUS
1985
Oak
24 x 24 x 36″

269 BRAUN SERIES 5317-30

HICKORY BUSINESS FURNITURE
1985
Designed by Wayne Braun
Maple frame, cherry surfaces
29 x 29½ x 34½″

**270 CAMBRIDGE SERIES
3068-10**

HICKORY BUSINESS FURNITURE
1986
Designed by Michael Vanderbuyl
Maple frame, cherry surfaces
23½ x 21 x 30½″

268

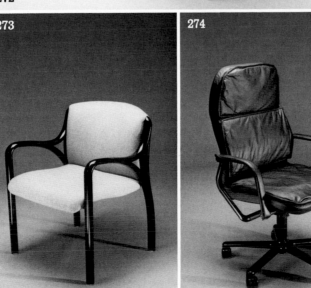

269

270 272

271 273 274

271 **SEDIA DE CONTRASTO
(CHAIR OF CONTRAST)**

THOMAS STAUFFER with
ALEKSANDRA WOYCZYNSKA
and PRESTON BUCHTEL
1985
Oiled walnut, leather, galvanized wire
36 x 24 x 30"

272 **CHALICE 7407-10**

HICKORY BUSINESS FURNITURE
1985
Designed by Orlando Diaz-Azcuy
Maple frame, cherry surfaces
28 x 25 x 31½"

273 **WINSOR WHITE**

VECTA CONTRACT
1986
Designed by Winsor White
Wood, fabric, foam
24½ x 27 x 32½"

274 **F.S. EXECUTIVE**

VECTA CONTRACT
1983
Designed by Franck & Sauer
Steel, aluminum, leather, foam
27½ x 27½ x 45½"

275 **HUDSON RIVER RUST-IC**

SID FLEISHER
1986
Scrap steel
15 x 18 x 30"

276 **ARCHIE**

LARRY KAGAN
1986
Steel, wood
15½ x 24 x 14"

277 **RICE CHAIR**

FRAN TAUBMAN
1986
Wood, stainless steel
31 x 31 x 26"

278 **SELANAOS**

CHRISTOPHER McMAHAN
1986
Ebonized ash, stainless steel
16½ x 21½ x 26½"

279 **BENUCCI SIDE CHAIR**

SARA JAFFE
1980
Honduras mahogany and rosewood,
aluminum
18 x 18 x 33"

280 **ARLO**

CUMBERLAND FURNITURE
CORP.
1986
Designed by Ulrich Bohme and
Wulf Schneider
Plywood (seat back), beechwood,
steel, chrome
23½ x 21½ x 31"

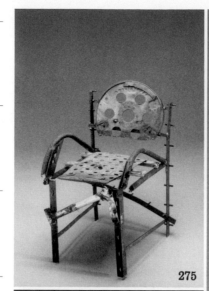

275

276 278

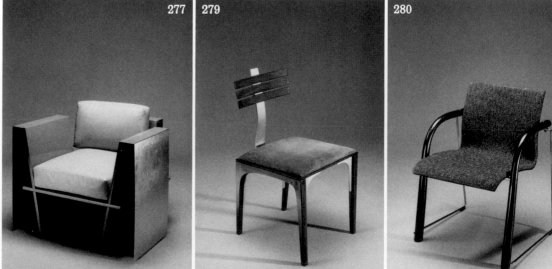

277 279 280

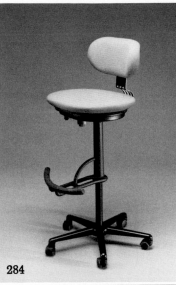

284

281 285

282

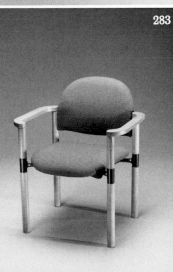

283

286

281 OHL 180

VECTA CONTRACT
1982
Designed by Herbert Ohl
Steel, nylon, leather
23¼ x 24½ x 31½"

282 UNNAMED

RICHARD WOLKOWITZ
1986
Wood, canvas
39 x 35 x 30"

283 CABAR CHAIR

JG FURNITURE SYSTEMS, INC.
1985
Wood, plywood, upholstery
24⅜ x 22⅝ x 31¾"

284 SPRINGBOK OPERATOR'S STOOL

JG FURNITURE SYSTEMS, INC.
1986
Designed by John Behringer
Plywood seat, back;
urethane foam; steel
19 x 19" (height adjusts)

285 SPRINGBOK TASK CHAIR

JG FURNITURE SYSTEMS, INC.
1986
Designed by John Behringer
Plywood seat, back;
urethane foam; steel
19 x 19 x 36"

286 CHAIR WITH KEVLAR SEAT

CHARLES SWANSON
1986
Baltic birch, plywood, Dacron-
covered Kevlar line
25 x 18 x 29"

71

287

290

293

288 291

294

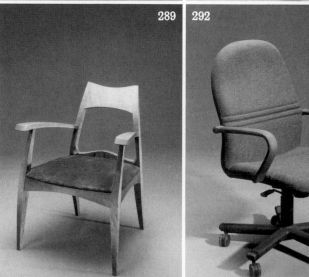

289 292

295

296

292 CONTURA 8600

THE GUNLOCKE COMPANY
1986
Designed by Robert Bernard Associates
Steel, molded polyurethane, upholstery
23¾ x 23 x 43″

293 BLACKSTONE

BRICKEL ASSOCIATES
1985
Designed by Ward Bennett for Brickel Associates
White ash, leather
23½ x 22½ x 33¾″

294 YOKE CHAIR

BRICKEL ASSOCIATES
1984
Designed by Ward Bennett for Brickel Associates
White ash, upholstery fabric
23¾ x 22½ x 30¼″

295 MANET CHAIR

GWEN WINSTON
1986
'Found' wrought iron chair, oil and latex paint
18 x 18 x 36″

296 CHAIR OF LIBRARY SCIENCE

EUGENE M. GEINZER
1984
Mahogany, beech
37¼ x 26½ x 28⅞″

297 GBI CHAIR

PAUL SEGAL ASSOCIATES
1986
Project Designer: George How
Cherry, birch, fabric
24 x 21 x 33¼"

298 SPLIT CIRCLE

ELIZABETH MARMOL
1986
Atelier Marmol
1986
Maple, ebony, black leather
17½ x 16 x 42"

299 TUMBLING BLOCK CHAIR

LYNNE PHIPPS
1986
Cherry, birch plywood
17 x 15 x 23"

300 BUILDING

MICHELE SAIE
1985
Steel
24 x 18 x 32"

301 JOE & PHIL

DANIEL LOUIS GOLDNER, RA
1985
Maple, mahogany veneer, fabric
15 x 15 x 17"

302 REC CHAIR

SYLVIA NETZER
1986
Cardboard display tube, silicon,
found objects
20 x 20 x 32"

297

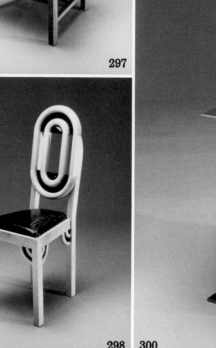

298

300

299 **301**

302

303

307

304

305

308

303 COURTHOUSE CHAIR 8401

THE GUNLOCKE COMPANY
1983
Designed by Walker/Group Inc.
Maple, walnut
22¼ x 23½ x 32″

304 JEFFERSON CHAIR

SUNARHAUSERMAN
1986
Designed by Niels Diffrient
Cast aluminum, urethane foam,
leather
29½ x 23¾ x 42¾″

305 ROTONDA CHAIR

SUNARHAUSERMAN
1980
Designed by Vignelli Designs
Steel frame, urethane foam,
fabric or leather
32¾ x 26 x 32″

306 GRAVES LOUNGE CHAIR

SUNARHAUSERMAN
1982
Designed by Michael Graves
Hardwood upholstery frame,
urethane foam, fabric or leather
32 x 29 x 28¾″

307 ERGON® LOW BACK

HERMAN MILLER, INC.
1976
Designed by Bill Stumpf
Cast aluminum, steel, polyurethane
and polypropylene foam
26½ x 23¼ x 42″

308 PROPER™ CHAIR

HERMAN MILLER, INC.
1986
Designed by Dragomir Ivicevic
Zinc, steel, black nickel,
polypropylene foam, polystyrene
18½ x 17 x 30″

309 **THE CHAIR**

TOM MUSORAFITA
1986
'Found' construction materials
(containers, sheetrock)
19 x 19 x 47"

310 **EQUA® LOW BACK**

HERMAN MILLER, INC.
1984
Designed by Bill Stumpf and
Don Chadwick
Rynite polyester resin, steel,
aluminum, polyurethane foam
23½ x 22½ x 36"

311 **CHAIR NO. 1**

ERIK KAAE ANDERSEN
1986
Lacquered hardwood, wool
damask upholstery
26½ x 26½ x 26½"

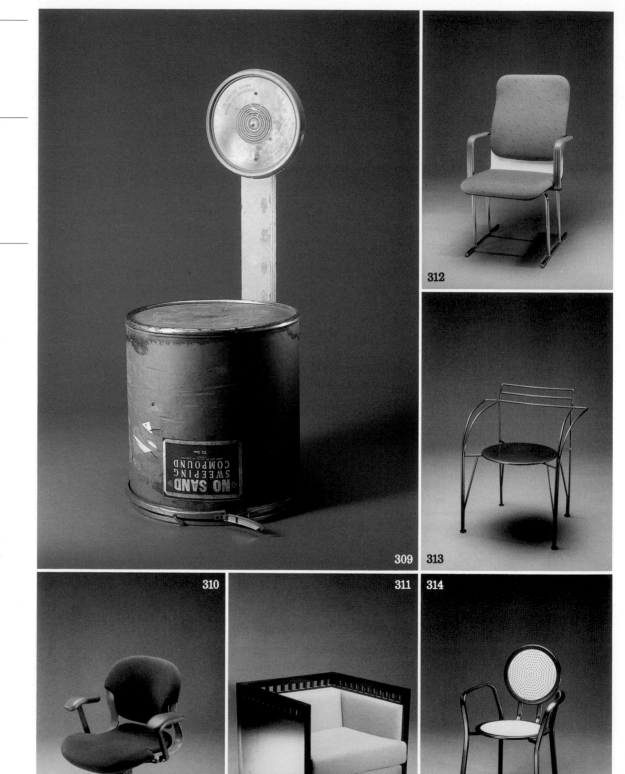

309

312

313

310

311

314

315

312 **SIRKUS HIGH BACK**

BEYLERIAN LIMITED
1984
Designed by Yrjo Kukkapuro
Birch plywood, plastic laminate,
tubular steel
17 x 24 x 38"

313 **LUNE D'ARGENT**

BEYLERIAN LIMITED
1985
Designed by Pascal Mourgue
Steel rod, polyester
textured-pewter finish
24 x 20 x 30"

314 **HALO**

BEYLERIAN LIMITED
1984
Designed by Franco Prioli
Tubular steel, steel plate,
rubber glides
21 x 18 x 33"

315 **KITCHEN CHAIR**

SYLVIA NETZER
1986
Steel tubes, silicon, found objects
16 x 16 x 32"

316

317 319

318 320

319   ARKURA [PROTOTYPE]

ALLEN H. BOWDEN
1986
Steel and enamel finish
20 x 20 x 48"

320   CEREMONIAL CHAIR

VICKI MOSS
1984
Courtesy of Ronald D. Abramson
Ash, leather
30 x 20 x 31"

321   ORBIT

JAMES EVANSON
1985
Wood, lacquer
36 x 36 x 33"

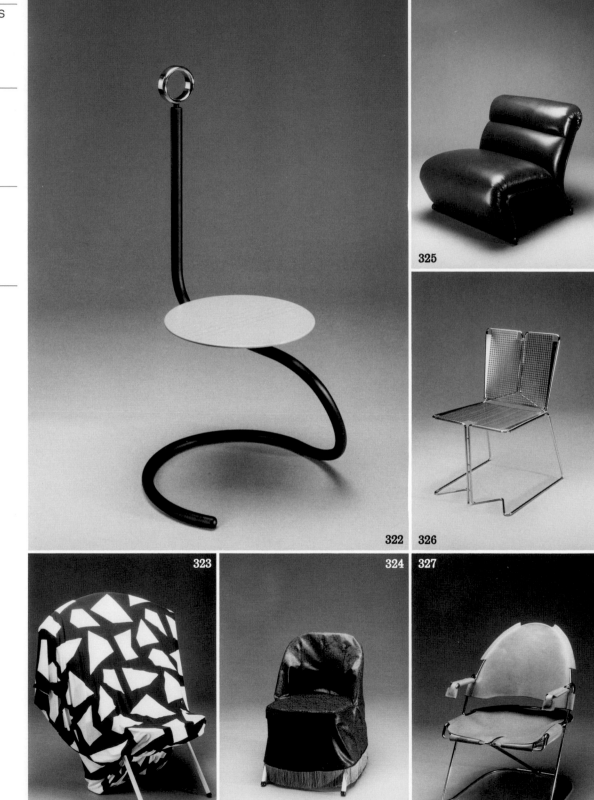

322 NOSHI

JO NAGAHARA & ASSOCIATES
1986
Stainless steel, aluminum
17¾ x 17¾ x 47¼"

323 MONTANA

P.D.Q.
Designed by Lee Hagen
1986
Steel, fabric
19 x 19 x 29½"

324 OHIO

P.D.Q.
Designed by Peter Schultz
1986
Steel, fabric
19 x 19 x 29½"

325 JAZZ SEATING

DAKOTA JACKSON, INC.
1983
Designed by Dakota Jackson
Lacquered bentwood, anodized
metal tubing, leather
30 x 36 x 30"

325

322   326

323   324   327

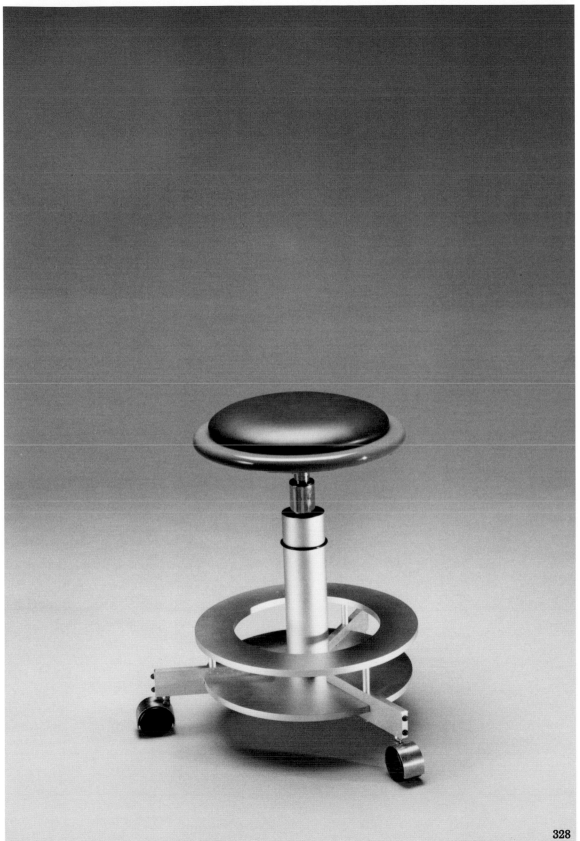

326 VADER

JONATHAN M. NELSON–
NISNEVICH DESIGN
1986
Produced by Acciaio, Inc.
Chromed steel, perforated metal
20 x 22 x 34″

327 TITI

JONATHAN M. NELSON–
NISNEVICH DESIGN
1985
Produced by Acciaio, Inc.
Chromed steel, leather
24 x 23 x 37″

328 SATURN STOOL

DAKOTA JACKSON, INC.
1977
Designed by Dakota Jackson
Satin anodized aluminum, leather,
lacquer rim
22 x 22 x 28″

329 DUO

ATELIER INTERNATIONAL, LTD.
1985
Designed by Werther Toffoloni
Beechwood, upholstery
19 x 20 x 34″

330 ARCHIZOOM

ATELIER INTERNATIONAL, LTD.
1979
Designed by
Archizoom Associates
Tubular steel, leather
22¾ x 22¾ x 34¼″

331 CAB

ATELIER INTERNATIONAL, LTD.
1979
Designed by Mario Bellini
Leather, steel
23½ x 20½ x 24½″

332 CHAIR TOWERS

MARY PEPCHINSKI
1984
Clear pine, brass screws
18 x 18 x 63½″

333 UNNAMED

BOB INGRAM
1986
Lacewood veneer, bubinga,
wool upholstery
28 x 25 x 34″

334 CHINA GOTHIC

JACK LARIMORE
1986
Hardwood frame, leather,
cotton/wool upholstery
28 x 30 x 34″

329

330

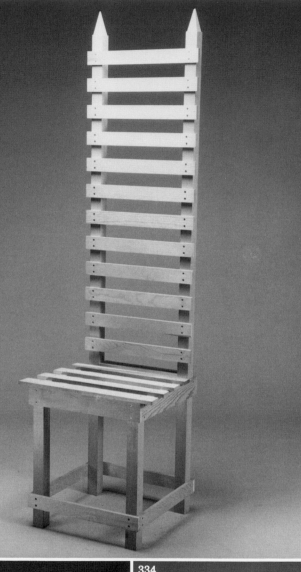

332

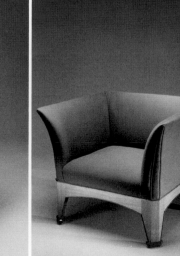

331 333

334

335

338

339

336   337   340

335 THE LIBERTY CHAIR

FREDERIC SCHWARTZ
1983
Anderson/Schwartz Architects
Hardwood, hand-rubbed lacquer
26 x 18 x 80″

336 LICOS CHAIR

HARRY C. WOLF, FAIA
1986
Wolf Associates Architects
Stainless steel, leather
21 x 21 x 27½″

337 GARDEN CHAIR

JAMES SCHRIBER
1986
Honduras mahogany, milk paint,
oil finish
31 x 27 x 31″

338 MERYL'S CHAIR
(A.K.A. HOUSE CHAIR)

FREDERIC SCHWARTZ
1985
Anderson/Schwartz Architects
Colorcore® on plywood
30 x 17½ x 41″

339 MYRA II

DAVID E. WOOLF
1985
Gertler & Woolf Architects
Purple heart, stainless steel
26 x 20 x 33″

340 NEW EMPIRE

JAMES EVANSON
1984
Wood, lacquer, Colorcore®
22 x 20 x 30″

341 UNNAMED

KALLE FAUSET
1986
Madrone burl, purple heart,
pau amarillo, ebonized walnut
30 x 26 x 30"

342 MYRA I

DAVID E. WOOLF
1985
Gertler & Woolf Architects
Purple heart, stainless steel
20½ x 20½ x 57"

343 COMET CLUB BARSTOOL

JAMES EVANSON
1985
Wood, lacquer, anodized aluminum
27 x 20 x 42"

344 SILHOUETTE CHAIR

ANTHONY TSIRANTONAKIS
1986
Lacquered wood, concrete, canvas
18 x 33 x 42"

341

342

343 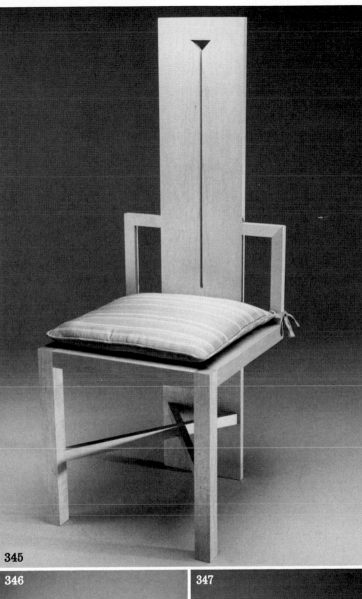 345

344 346 347

345 **SPENCER**

JEAN BAPTISTE DUCRUET
1986
Maple, silk (Boris Kroll)
18 x 18 x 48¾"

346 **CHICESTER CLUB CHAIR**

DONGHIA
1978
Designed by Angelo Donghia
Wood, upholstery
42 x 36 x 33"

347 **ITANOLD CHAIR
(SLAB CHAIR)**

PAT SAPINSLEY
1985
Built by Luna Cabinetworks Inc.
Bird's-eye maple, black ash,
aluminum, silk, down
17 x 17 x 36"

348 STRASBURG

BERNHARDT INDUSTRIES
1986
Designed by Don Alguire
Maple
24 x 24½ x 33½"

349 FAN CHAIR

PAUL GESHLIDER
1985
Aluminum, rope, 5 boxer fans
18 x 20 x 36"

350 TRIESTE

TUOHY FURNITURE
CORPORATION
1986
Designed by Daniel Cramer
Hardwood, mahogany,
wool broadcloth
24¼ x 24 x 31½"

351 COMO

BERNHARDT INDUSTRIES
1986
Designed by Don Alguire
Maple
21½ x 24 x 32¾"

352 LAMBDA II

TUOHY FURNITURE
CORPORATION
1978
Designed by Bernard Tuohy
Red oak, foam padding,
wool homespun
22 x 23 x 32"

353 RS48 LOUNGE CHAIR

NIENKÄMPER
1986
Stainless steel, nylon mesh,
foam, leather
26 x 29 x 26½"

351

348

352

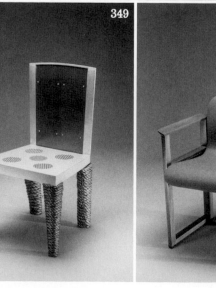

349

350

353

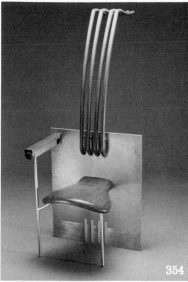

354

355

357

356

358

359

354 C.HAIR-1

MAKOTO WATANABE
1986
Laminated wood, aluminum
23½ x 31½ x 59"

355 C.HAIR-2

MAKOTO WATANABE
1986
Laminated wood
19¾ x 20½ x 59"

356 UNNAMED

CRISTINA M. BOCOBO
1985
Cherry, stained glass
23 x 20 x 60"

357 SUMMIT

BERNHARDT INDUSTRIES
1986
Designed by Don Alguire
Hardwood frame, upholstered
27 x 26 x 31¾"

358 UNNAMED

ROSS ANDERSON
1981
Anderson/Schwartz Architects
Plywood, wood studs
36 x 36 x 60"

359 UNNAMED

JAMES BRITLAND
1981
Red oak, velvet
22½ x 24½ x 37"

360 Z-BLOCKI

PAUL FITTING &
ASSOCIATES, INC.
1986
Designed by Ira Ballen
Plastic laminate, fabric
30 x 30 x 36″

361 CHAIR/TABLE

ROBERT C. WHITLOCK
1980
Maple, birch plywood
26 x 26 x 40″

362 THE HANDKERCHIEF CHAIR

KNOLL INTERNATIONAL
1985
Designed by Vignelli Designs
Glass fiber-reinforced, molded
polyester shell, wire frame
23 x 22½ x 29″

363 BLACK DIAMOND

CARL TESE
1984
Plywood, auto lacquer,
perforated metal
20 x 18 x 34½″

364 SAPPER ADVANCED HIGH-BACK CHAIR

KNOLL INTERNATIONAL
1979
Designed by Richard Sapper
Cast aluminum, steel,
polyurethane, upholstery
26¾ x 27½ x 38½″

365 SCHULTZ ARMCHAIR

KNOLL INTERNATIONAL
1981
Designed by M. Richard Schultz
Tubular steel frame; vinyl,
leather, fabric
21¾ x 20⅛ x 32″

360

361 363

362 364 365

366

367

368

369

370

371

372 **ARCHIE BUNKER ON MARS**

VINCENT CIULLA/
PAUL NARKIEWICZ
1986
Vincent Ciulla Design
Associates, Inc.
Plywood, pine, fabric,
paper, metal, etc.
36 x 32 x 36"

373 **URBANE ARM**

DONGHIA
1986
Designed by John Hutton
Birch, upholstery
22 x 25½ x 34"

374 **MADISON OCCASIONAL CHAIR**

DONGHIA
1981
Designed by John Hutton
Maple, upholstery
29 x 31 x 30"

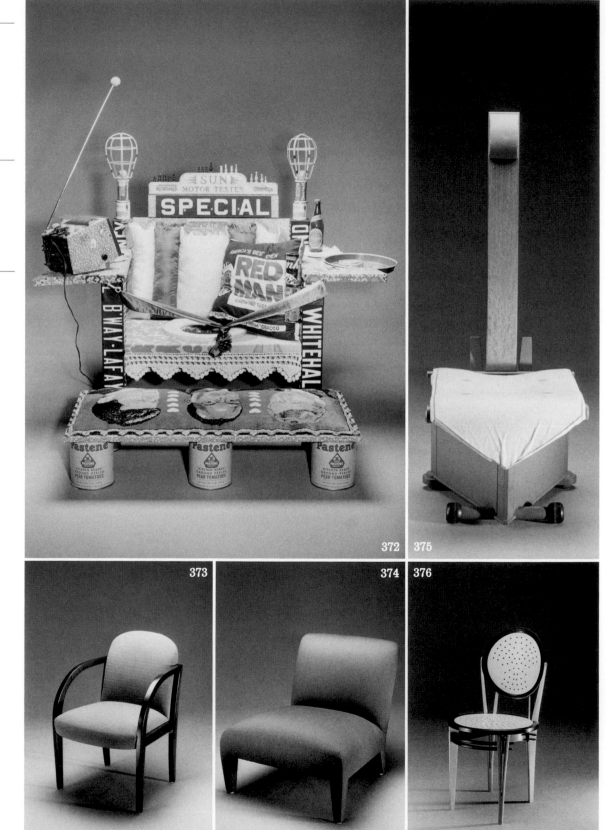

372 375

373 374 376

377

375   DINER

GREGG DRAUDT
1985
Oak, maple, lacquer, cotton, foam
17 x 18 x 48″

376   MOON CHAIR

KALLE FAUSET
1984
Courtesy of Ronald D. Abramson
Holly, purple heart, bloodwood,
ebonized walnut
17 x 17 x 34″

377   RIART ROCKING CHAIR

CARLOS RIART
1982
Manufactured by Knoll International
American holly or ebony frame
24¾ x 32½ x 39¼″

378 UNNAMED

JONATHAN H. MOELLER
1986
Hardwood laminate, Masonite
30 x 36 x 42"

379 MONICA

CONDE HOUSE
1986
Designed by Richard Schultz
Laminated cherry, plywood
panels, leather
33 x 33¼ x 30½"

380 RICARDO

CONDE HOUSE
1986
Designed by Richard Schultz
Steel tubing, maple
21¼ x 23½ x 32"

**381 BÜHK 100
MANAGEMENT CHAIR**

ALLSTEEL, INC.
1986
Designed by Peter Bühk
Aluminum, molded urethane,
elastomeric tilt spring
23⅜ x 24½ x 40⅞"

382 BÜHK 100 SIDE CHAIR

ALLSTEEL INC.
1986
Designed by Peter Bühk
Aluminum, molded urethane
23⅜ x 24⅜ x 32¹⁄₁₆"

**383 BÜHK 100
OPERATIONAL CHAIR**

ALLSTEEL INC.
1986
Designed by Peter Bühk
Aluminum, molded urethane,
elastomeric tilt spring
23 x 24½ x 38¾"

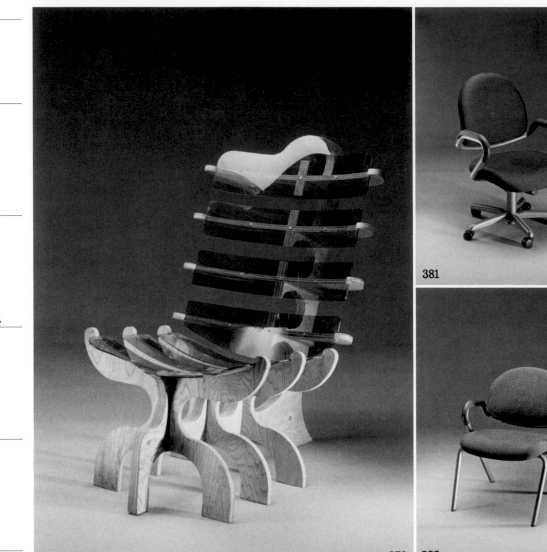

381

378   382

379   380   383

384

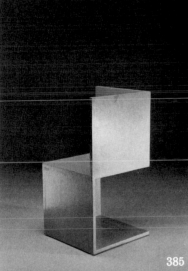

385

387

386

388   389

384 CONCRETE CHAIR

DAVID HERTZ
1982
Syndesis Studio, Inc.
Concrete, cowhide, casters
14 x 18 x 33"

385 THE BLUE CHAIR

HUNG-SHU HU
1982
Wood, epoxy paint
16 x 16 x 32"

386 ORIGAMI CHAIR

TAKEFUMI AIDA
1985
Wood, paint
17¾ x 17¾ x 35½"

387 THE LAP

HUNG-SHU HU
1985
Wood, epoxy paint
16½ x 16¼ x 31"

388 WALNUT DINING CHAIR

SANDY VOLKMANN
1982
American walnut, ebony wedges,
oil finish
20 x 19 x 37"

389 CHERRY SIDE CHAIR

SANDY VOLKMANN
1983
Cherry, maple splats,
pressed cane seat
18 x 17 x 37"

390